THE
CLAIRVOYANT
PATH

About the Author

Michelle DesPres is a clairvoyant medium focusing her insight on the empowerment of individuals and communities. She provides conscious innovative information and tools that enable individuals to create a life worthy of their unique potential.

Trained as a clairvoyant through a school formulated after the Berkeley Psychic Institute's clairvoyant program, she is now teaching techniques designed to foster your psychic healing and development.

In addition to reading for clients, teaching classes, and hosting dialogues, Michelle also provides a seasonal energetic forecast designed to better enable her clients and students to stay in flow with the specific energies of the time.

To Write to the Author

If you wish to contact the author or would like more information about this book, please write to the author in care of Llewellyn Worldwide Ltd. and we will forward your request. Both the author and publisher appreciate hearing from you and learning of your enjoyment of this book and how it has helped you. Llewellyn Worldwide Ltd. cannot guarantee that every letter written to the author can be answered, but all will be forwarded. Please write to:

Michelle DesPres
℅ Llewellyn Worldwide
2143 Wooddale Drive
Woodbury, MN 55125-2989

Please enclose a self-addressed stamped envelope for reply,
or $1.00 to cover costs. If outside the U.S.A., enclose
an international postal reply coupon.

Many of Llewellyn's authors have websites with additional information and resources. For more information, please visit our website at http://www.llewellyn.com.

Michelle DesPres

THE
CLAIRVOYANT
PATH

Follow Your Inner Wisdom to
Healing, Empowerment & Change

Llewellyn Publications
Woodbury, Minnesota

FIRST EDITION
First Printing, 2012

Book design by Bob Gaul
Cover art © Stock 4B/PunchStock
Cover design by Lisa Novak
Interior Art: Llewellyn Art Department
Editing by Amy Quale

Llewellyn Publications is a registered trademark of Llewellyn Worldwide Ltd.

Library of Congress Cataloging-in-Publication Data (**Pending**)
ISBN: 978-0-7387-3018-9

Llewellyn Publications
A Division of Llewellyn Worldwide Ltd.
2143 Wooddale Drive
Woodbury, MN 55125-2989
www.llewellyn.com

Printed in the United States of America

Contents

Part IV: The Influences that Make Up Your Perspective

Part V: Reinventing Yourself

Acknowledgments

To "My Three Sons": Oh, if only growing up was really like a 1960s sitcom, right? Jerry, Sam, and Kyle, because of you all, I have love, acceptance, and understanding. Semper Fi and Family Pride ... welcome to the mix, Kris.

To my dad: Thanks for loving me.

To my mom: Thanks for letting me go.

To my sister Rena: Thanks for always being you and for loving me unconditionally.

To Ray Sedillo: Thank you for bringing back into my life a love of reading and writing. This is a dream come true.

To Shauna Smith Troxell: Our sisterhood means the world to me. Thanks for understanding who I was and for helping me become who I am. You're a master at walking the talk ... the one thing I admire most in a person. You are a rare gem. I'm so happy to have been brought into your fold.

To Lauryn Stiner: Thank you for teaching me the art of enjoyment, and for getting me out of my head and into the world. You are wise beyond your years.

To Brian Lindstrom: I owe my creative force and drive for this project to the unwavering faith and love you gave me. Heaven knows how to put the right people in the right place at the right time.

To Kelly Hallenbeck: You have always been a source of encouragement and truth. I appreciate your insights and I'm thrilled to have family like you in my life.

To Calie Pierce: Thank you for tediously reading rough draft after rough draft; your dedication and belief in me set the example of persistence I would follow.

To Carrie Obry and Sandy Sullivan: Thank you for helping me find the formula! It wouldn't have worked without you.

To Julie Luckey: Your kindness, gentleness, and insight were keys that kept me moving through this process. I eternally thank you.

To Thursday Night Clairvoyant Class: Here's to still going strong. I love you ladies!

To my clients: Your support has been my foundation. It's been a pleasure to see the world through such amazing people.

To the Semper Fi Fund, Bethesda Navel Hospital, Balboa Naval Hospital, and the men and women like Kristen Valent-Sedillo who are the heroes who keep the heroes alive. Thank you for your service. You are a true inspiration.

*To the end of time as we know it
and the beginning of life as we love it.*

Introduction:
Why I Wrote This Book

No man is free who is not a master of himself.

—Epictetus

W e've all heard the saying, "kill them with kindness," but do you really think kindness can kill? Perhaps we have it backward. Maybe you can't literally kill someone else with kindness, but what if it could kill you? Kindness can be a double-edged sword. Being kind can make you feel like you've contributed something positive to the world and are making a difference, or it can make you feel as though you have given yourself away to the world by always accommodating everyone else in lieu of doing what is right for you. Most of my life I was far too kind— not wanting to disappoint anyone and always wanting to live up to every- one's expectations. Unfortunately, that type of stress-filled kindness was causing me to experience heart palpitations, stomach issues, and a type of depression that was tearing me apart. Then I learned how to use my clairvoyant abilities to better discern all kinds of things, such as when my kindness was creating genuine joy in the world versus when my kindness was subtly killing me. With this greater knowledge, I learned how and when to be kind to others and how and when to be true to myself. Later, I established my clairvoyant practice as a way of relaying this inner knowledge to others so they too could learn how to access and share in this greater discernment and ultimate empowerment over their lives. Now I offer it to you in the form of this book.

The main reason I wrote this book was to provide a reference guide for understanding the science of the higher clairvoyant senses and how we can consciously operate them to create our reality. What you receive in this text is far more expansive and comprehensive than what my clients receive, as the messages are now conveniently bundled in one tome. Instead of having multiple sessions with me regarding the nature of this material, you now have access to it all whenever you need it.

Also included in this book is a higher understanding regarding the cycle of time that earth and humanity are traversing, and why we consider climate change and 2012 to be the ultimate "end times." These are pivotal times indeed, and our higher senses are the keys to our survival. Unfortunately, most of us assume we have no control over these circumstances, when in truth we hold all the cards, and the power is squarely in our hands to either create devastation or create peace. This leads me to another reason I wrote this book: to help educate people about how to alter their personal energetic climates to be in alignment with healing and well-being, and to transform their lives into something meaningful.

Along with providing a higher understanding of who we are and what the times are prompting us to become, this book also serves to introduce the idea of a re-education that focuses on the new science of quantum relating to the cure to humanity's ills. Quantum science is confirming that it is the spirit of our thoughts that inevitably manifests into physical form. Therefore, as our thoughts create form, thoughts of destruction create chaos, while thoughts of cooperation create peace. Suddenly the greatest revelation of our day is that our inner reality creates our outward experiences, suggesting that we as spirits absolutely have control over the outcome of our lives. Should we balance our inward upheaval, we need never experience its chaos in our outward reality. In that sense, end-times prophecies only serve as a marker for what *might* ensue should we not seek inner resolution. However, should we seek inner resolution, the end times gets a whole lot prettier. This leads me to the greatest reason I wrote this book: to provide a reference manual and complete curriculum for exploring your quantum self from inception to manifestation so you can begin to create a life in alignment with the intentions of your spirit.

How to Use This Book

This book is unique in that it provides intimate stores, in-depth theories, and progressive exercises for understanding your inner climate, as well as instruction for how we can affect those climates with the intent of creating a new status quo during these shifting times. Although I am a trained clairvoyant under Lewis Bostwick's philosophies for developing insight, what I teach and share as theories and exercises are only loosely based on Bostwick's program. Over the years of working with clients and students, I have adapted the techniques to accommodate the ever-shifting lifestyles of people today. This allows us to expand outside of our spiritual bubble and begin living as a spirit in our everyday lives. The stories, insights, and exercises found in this book offer a revolutionary and innovative look at the subject of energetic climate change while covering the myriad of concepts involved in living as a spirit in a body today.

The best way to use this book is by first recognizing that it is laid out into five parts. Part I introduces you to the new education of inner wisdom, quantum magnetics, and affecting change within your reality. The exercises found in part one serve as the basics, or foundation, for all the other exercises while at the same time providing you with an understanding of your clairvoyant abilities and how they operate within the quantum field.

As you move on to Part II, your perspective will expand, giving you a greater understanding of your soul, its totality, and your higher purpose. The exercises in this section are designed to help you learn to maintain and balance your personal magnetics as you become more aware of the bigger picture of your personal soul history.

With Part III, you will begin exploring your soul's greater design as you discover the purpose of your growth and evolution. The clairvoyant exercises in the section provide you with techniques for taking ownership of your personal energy field as you begin enacting a life worthy of your uniqueness.

In Part IV, you begin to investigate the many traits and behaviors that unconsciously influence you at any given moment and how to recognize their intent and effect on you. The clairvoyant exercises in this section teach you how to view these behaviors for the sake of managing their influences in your life.

Lastly, Part V wraps the concepts together by demonstrating the ways in which our spirits and bodies can become healed, empowered, and changed. These exercises give you an understanding of how to take charge of your personal healing, set intentions toward your empowered future, and spark inspiration in ways you never thought of before.

You will notice as you read that each story, theory, and exercise can be inwardly explored over longer cycles of time. This book also serves as a reference guide that can be revisited once you have learned how to walk the clairvoyant path and can notice the concepts as they recycle in your life.

The Clairvoyant Path

What does it mean to walk the clairvoyant path? For me, it meant being willing to set aside my fears and doubts about psychic abilities (which I didn't think I had) while at the same time being willing to be adventurous and brave even in the face of uncertainty. It led me to a greater understanding of my true nature. As a clairvoyant, I have come to remember myself as a visionary and a revolutionary, a shaman and a martyr, a victim and an aggressor. This awareness has forever altered my perception of my inner self, my role within humanity, and my purpose on earth today.

However, I wasn't always clairvoyant, at least not consciously. I certainly grew up having distinct clairvoyant (psychic) moments, as have we all, but I never really thought I was anything special. On the contrary, I thought I was very ordinary and dull. In the end, it would turn out that I was right—I wasn't anything special. The fact is that we are all clairvoyant. It's more about recognizing instead of denying and developing instead of ignoring what amounts to our innate intuitive faculty. Yet there lies the problem—how does a person go about exploring and developing their intuitive faculty if they were never told that part of them even existed? This is the issue we all face today and is consequently why we are in need of a re-education.

For me, this re-education began after experiencing a series of crises in my life that led me to seeking a higher or spiritual understanding of my circumstances. This is generally how most of us are launched into a spiritual awakening: we experience something traumatic that causes us to question our being. In my quest to define my spiritual reality, I come across a school in Denver called the Inner Insight Institute based on Lewis Bostwick's clairvoyant program. There I would learn the art of personal empowerment through fostering my communications with my inner spirit and the spirits of those around me.

As I clairvoyantly explored the realms of my spirit, I quickly recognized the vastness of this quantum space. For the first time, I witnessed myself as pure energy that was connected to a part of everything surrounding me. I recognized that I was grounded to this planet yet I was present in the heavens as well. I saw that I had both earthly and universal energy currents running through me, as well as feminine and masculine currents of energy. I became aware that my energy ran through a system of generators called *chakras*, and that the light emitting from the chakras was ultimately that which made up my physical reality. And I also came to realize that I could change the light frequency that was emitting from my chakras, and in so doing I could change my reality.

However, the most empowering thing I learned at school was that I was in agreement with all my circumstances—good, bad, or indifferent—and therefore, I was the only one responsible for my perceived limitations and victimizations. If I did not acknowledge and ultimately change the agreements that kept me disempowered, then I could expect the same patterns of hoping for change only to find failure. This meant I had to break the mold within which I had been living. I had to look at who I had been, who I was currently, and who I aspired to be. I had to summon the courage to change that which no longer served my highest good, and I had to find the determination to live authentically from the perspective of my heart. This is what it means to walk the clairvoyant path.

I have been walking the clairvoyant path now for many years. I even made it my career, though it is not so much a career as it is a lifestyle. Although I still experience struggle and turmoil at times, I now have peace of mind in knowing that all I have to do is change perspectives and my reality changes too; to be sure, today is all about changing realities. Over the many years I have worked as a clairvoyant, I have come to realize that we live in pivotal times in which it is imperative we recognize the metaphor that earth's climate change is a signal that humanity must change its climate and create a different reality.

Some would say that our country is in need of a revolution, yet there is already a revolution afoot. It is not a revolution of nations and of men; it is not a revolution of blood and of conquest. Rather, it is a revolution of time and of age, and it is a revolution of spirit and of matter. It is the revolution of the lands and the waters, the plants and the animals. It is the revolution of the earth herself as the cycle of time has come for her to shift her climates. The earth is evolving and expanding into a new way of being that we have never before experienced on this planet. As the earth shifts her climate, it is a signal that all living things must shift as well, so perhaps this revolution is more of a revelation for humanity as today sparks the re-evaluation of our being.

Energetic Climate Change:
The Reinvention of Humanity

When a client comes to see me for a reading, they are generally curious about their relationships, money, career, and health. Yet, once these individual issues are addressed, the next questions on everyone's minds are, *What is happening to planet earth?* and *What does 2012 really mean?* The truth is nobody knows with absolutely certainty what the future holds for humanity and planet earth. When I am asked these questions, the only source I can turn to is Gaia (the goddess who birthed the sea, sky, and mountains of which we call earth). What I have come to know is that there is another complimentary theory yet to be explored regarding climate change and the end times that ultimately leads to the transformation of our being.

As I have viewed earth's "future" and spoken to Gaia, earth's spirit, I have learned that earth is moving from one great world age into another great world age, and that the patterns of time are changing. We can think of it like this: time is not linear, it is cyclical as it waves in cycles that ebb and flow in a never-ending spiral. Sometimes we are brought around to our past, and sometimes we are tossed out into the future. The trick ultimately becomes learning how to live in the present. In that sense, time is movement and rotation, just as twenty-four hours equals one day's rotation of the planet, three hundred and sixty-five days equals one year's rotation around the sun. Many ancient cultures from all over the world held deeper understandings of the greater cycles and rhythms of time. In the book *The 2012 Story: The Myths, Fallacies, and Truth Behind the Most*

Intriguing Date in History, author John Major Jenkins explains how the Maya knew that every twenty-six thousand years our sun leads the planets into alignment with the core, or central axis, of the Milky Way galaxy. On December 21, 2012, this processional year's rotation will take place marking the halfway point of the sun's full rotation around the galactic center. However, what is even more curious about this time is that while the sun is making its rare journey through the central axis, the earth is also reaching a pivotal juncture in her rotations around the sun. As the sun is marking the beginning and ending of a period of time, the earth is also commemorating the beginning of a new world age.

As it stands now, the earth is exiting and entering a new 5,125-year rotation around the sun, thus marking the ending of one world age and the beginning of another world age for planet earth. Both the current "end times" and "2012" phenomena are based on the idea of a shifting world age coming to full rotation. However, the one factor that seems to get lost in all the hubbub and doomsday rants about climate change and the end times is the magnetic impact that these rare alignments have upon the core of the sun and earth, and how that ultimately leads to humanity's energetic alteration.

As the sun and the earth move through their rare processional alignments, their magnetic cores are altered as they begin to resonate at a new frequency and vibration. Gaia explained it to me like this:

> *It's like pumping a sound frequency through a water droplet and watching the geometric formation that takes shape and dances to the rhythm. As the frequency increases, like we are seeing today, the droplet alters its formation, creating more and more complex shapes and formations with each accession in tone.*

The sun's and earth's magnetic cores can be likened to the droplet dancing to a new and higher frequency as they realign into a new world age formation. Subsequently, as our life-giving forces of sun and earth energetically attune to a new vibration, all living things must also attune themselves to the same higher frequency. But just how do we go about attuning ourselves to this higher vibrational world age? First, we have to recognizing earth's greater plan and design in order to know what we can do today.

Through my many years of reading the earth and her world ages, I have become familiar with her design and the purpose that she serves. While this may be our first time consciously going through a world age shift, it certainly isn't earth's first time around the block, which is exactly the reason she has a very well-designed plan for her new cycle of time. As Gaia explains it, earth is a dualistic planet designed to abundantly sustain life while holding a foundation for cultivating balance and peace for herself and all her creatures, including humanity. I have to say, I sort of snickered when I heard this because it didn't seem to me that earth was maintaining balance and peace; quite the contrary. However, Gaia continued explaining that prior to her plan coming to fruition, earth would have to first experience the antithesis of her goal to achieve her ultimate purpose.

It seems earth would first have to cycle through a 5,125-year period known as the matriarchal world age in which the feminine nature would be seeded upon the planet, followed by another 5,125-year period known as the patriarchal world age in which the masculine nature would be seeded upon the planet. Although the time of women was like a garden of spirit and light, it was out of balance in that it only honored the feminine abilities and disregarded the power and beauty of the masculine. Yet as life has a way of evening itself out, the patriarchal world age would soon take over as the cycle of time shifted into an honoring of the masculine abilities and a disregarding of the feminine power and beauty, which is the time period we live in now but are cycling out of with 2012.

The great thing about this time is that we have reached that moment when the world ages are shifting yet again. Earth has anchored a feminine pole and she has anchored a masculine pole, and now for the first time ever, earth can hold her balance, fulfilling her destiny and purpose. Subsequently, humanity must now follow earth's lead and learn to shift its energetic nature to reflect the balance of the times. But don't be fooled, there is yet another paradox that must be flipped if we truly wish to achieve sustainable balance at this time. What I mean is sustainable balance and peace do not come from rectifying our *outward* relationships to the things in our lives, it first must be found by seeking the *inward* balance of our own personal masculine and feminine quantum natures. Do you see the paradox? Peace doesn't actually come by rectifying our differences with others—it comes by rectifying our differences with ourselves first. Once we are conscious of our own inner balance, we naturally begin to treat the world around us differently. As we become more loving and accepting of ourselves, we become more loving and accepting of others, and suddenly the world around us begins to reflect our peaceful and balanced state of mind.

It is generally recognized that industrialized society is at a crisis point. Choices relating to energy, environment, control of technology, overpopulation, unemployment, land use, government roles, and business roles all seem to indicate that we need a fundamental change in direction. Luckily, with these pivotal times we can now transform and repattern our past of greed, war, manipulation, and separation into a higher cycle of cooperation, acceptance, abundance, and joy—simply by balancing our individual climates and allowing that balance to be reflected in the world.

Now is the perfect time to consider reinventing our lives while a new world design is just beginning to establish. We have a rare and unique opportunity to change our personal energetic climates, which eventually changes the social, political, financial, and philosophical climates of the world. So contemplate this for a while: What do you want your life to be? What do you want your relationships to feel like? What do you want the world to reflect? What type of pattern will you establish with earth's new 5,125-year era of time?

Clairvoyance:
The Tool of the New World Age

The solution to our life's issues is really a simple fix. It simply takes a willingness to imagine a time when the natural forces of wind, sun, and water will provide us with free energy, communications, and technologies. It takes a willingness to envision living locally, learning to develop our personal relationships, spending more time with our families and loved ones, and interacting globally in harmony with those around us. Yet along with all of the above, we must also be willing to embrace the tool of the new world age.

Every great period of time has its tools; the Stone Age had stone, and the Bronze Age had bronze. This new world age can be likened to the clairvoyant age in which our greatest tool is our ability to communicate inwardly with our spirit and to outwardly recognize and honor the spirit in others. Clairvoyance is a discipline of the sixth sense, which allows us to heal our limitations and manifest our intentions into reality. We can use our clairvoyance to observe our intentions and our beliefs as we learn to take responsibility over our creations. We can use our higher vision to witness our individual soul's plan, better enabling us to consciously choose how to express our free will. And we can use our higher perspective to discover what drives our nature and why we pattern and project our individually unique circumstances. We can even use our clairvoyance to view our bodies, spirits, emotions, and minds as we learn to reclaim our power to heal ourselves as we transform our ways of being.

There is a universal magic available to us in the form of a higher sense. The earth's new world age requires that we learn to harness this infinite magic by evolving our sciences into an understanding of the quantum realms of the body and the spirit. Clairvoyance is the tool that allows humankind to take advantage of its greatest hour. The only question is, are we aware of what the hour demands? The hour calls for higher perspective of the soul and its totality and multidimensionality. The hour calls for reconciliation of our karma and what it has created in our lives. More than anything, the hour calls for exploring our spirits and claiming our rightful positions as the cocreators of our reality. There are fundamental truths that must be re-initiated and taught to us as the tools for the new world age, and so the hour also calls for us to seek a new education. Luckily there is a new science that can be embraced as the tool for the shifting age. It is the science of the higher clairvoyant senses that teaches us how to become healed and empowered as we begin to live as a spirit in a body, which may very well be the pinnacle achievement and purpose of the human condition.

PART I

The New Education of Inner Wisdom

1

You Have
Inner
Wisdom

Going to school for the first time was a big event for me. I was a naturally curious kid who enjoyed exploring new people, places, and things. Leading up to those first days of school, my imagination was running wild thinking about all the new experiences I would be having. I imagined learning to read and write, add and subtract; I envisioned singing in music class and painting in art class; and I anticipated making friends with all of my new classmates. Imagine my surprise when what I envisioned turned out to be nothing like the reality I would experience. When it came right down to it, my beginning years in elementary school would wound me in ways I was not prepared for and teach me lessons I wasn't expecting.

Kindergarten was a breeze if not a bit redundant. The two years before school, I spent my days watching *Sesame Street* and learning to write my name, the alphabet, and the numbers. My teacher was naturally impressed and I was instantly her pet. But you know how the saying goes, "You don't know what you got till it's gone." Soon the class tables would turn and I would find I was on the opposite end of the curve.

Although I could write all the letters and numbers, when it came to reading (which was new for me) the letters all seemed to jump around and switch places. Consequently, it took me a little longer to formulate my thoughts and correctly say it out loud. Unfortunately, even as a child, time was a luxury I wasn't afforded as I was quickly labeled a "slow" reader by my teachers—a classification that would have a severe impact on my childhood psyche. Whenever class would break into reading groups, I would be taken out and sent to an isolated area with other "slow" readers. Over time I became more and more embarrassed each time I was pulled out of class. I felt ashamed of myself for not being good enough, and soon my shame caused me to disengage not only from my teachers and the institute of school, but I disengaged from the other kids as well. As a result, one girl in particular would pick on me and tell me I was stupid. It was a classic case of bullying. The school had labeled me "different," and my being considered a "slow" reader made me a target. And then as if things couldn't get any worse, school would throw me another curve ball.

In the first grade when we started learning to write in cursive, my handwriting slanted to the left when it was supposed to slant to the right, and often times I transposed letters and numbers as if my brain worked backward (a distinction some might say still exists for me today). It seemed that not only was I a slow reader, but apparently I couldn't write correctly, either. There I was, once again being called out on my inability to perform on command, making my school life all that more exasperating. How did everyone else seem to do everything right while I did everything wrong? I walked before I crawled, I couldn't remember my left from my right, and I spoke when I was only supposed to be spoken to. I began to think my bully was justified in calling me "stupid." Then one day something stirred inside me that would alter my elementary life forever.

One wintry morning prior to school, all the children were huddled together at the front doors waiting to be let into the building. My bully was behind me. She was calling me names and pulling my hair (all her normal ploys) and although I tried to ignore her annoyances, it only fueled her persistence. It was then that something inside me made me question myself. Did I really believe I was stupid? My heart screamed out NO! I didn't believe I was stupid. I knew how to read and I knew how to write—I simply had my own way of doing it.

It was then that from out of nowhere I thought, *How stupid is she to be pulling my hair while I'm holding a metal lunchbox?* Without a doubt, I knew I was smart enough to take matters into my own hands and change my destiny. I was cold, frustrated, and fed up in general. Without a second thought and with all my certainty and knowingness, I turned around swinging my metal Scooby Doo lunchbox at my bully, hitting her square in the face and breaking her nose. I spent the next several hours sitting outside the principal's office listening to her mother yell.

Today, being a mother of three sons, I understand that children generally learn boundaries by first lashing out at their environments. That's exactly what I did that day, and it was nothing I would ever do again. I felt horrible—I had really hurt her. I had never been pushed to my limit like that before, and I never once thought about the pain I would be inflicting as it somehow seemed to match my own internal pain and frustration. All I wanted was the same respect the other kids were getting, and I instinctively knew how to make that happen.

In the end, I may not have been able to change the structure of my education to fit my needs, but I could certainly change the way I allowed people to treat me. What could have resulted in years of torment and bullying was certainly averted in my moment of knowingness. Never again did my bully pick on me or anyone else. Over time, the two of us even became close friends. More importantly, I stopped being introverted and learned to start interacting with my peers, saving me from becoming a complete social outcast and recluse. Still, the most important lesson I learned on that day was that no matter what I might be experiencing in my life, I could take charge and alter my circumstances at any moment—all I had to do was listen to my own inner wisdom and follow my knowingness with appropriate boundaries.

Envisioning the New Education of Inner Wisdom

Today I find myself yet again needing to stand up for what is right and fair in regards to education and individuality. With our energetically shifting climate, we are offered an opportunity to begin honoring the innate diversity in every individual by simply re-educating ourselves about our spirits, their connectedness, and the magic of their complexities.

Ask any kid today if they would like to attend the Hogwarts School of Witchcraft and Wizardry or the Xavier Institute for Higher Learning, and you will hear a resounding *YES*. The crazy thing is fictional "gifted" schools like these will likely be a reality in the very near future. I recently saw an interview with world-renowned theoretical physicist Dr. Michio Kaku where he stated that it was his belief that within the next fifteen years teleportation, telekinesis, and telepathy will be our children's reality given the discoveries now being made in the quantum sciences. You know what this means? Schools like Hogwarts and Xavier Institute aren't just fictional schools for wizards and wolverines anymore, because it seems we now understand that every person has the magic of the universe inside them.

I already work with many magical children who have their heightened clairvoyant senses fully intact. My sister Annette has one of these children. From the very beginning, Rain was experiencing clairvoyant phenomenon. She would follow objects that no one else would see, and talk to people no one else could hear as she was already encountering her own quantum reality with spirits and "otherworldly" things. But never before had her insights been more relevant than the day she helped her mother and I dissipate a very desperately brewing tension.

One morning I woke up recalling a dream I had just had about Annette and myself in which we were teaching a class with a poisonous snake. Although this was certainly a known hazard of the class, the snake was unusually out of control and I worried it might attack one of the students. I quickly looked around to see a frazzled Annette; she was franticly trying to accommodate all the students' worries and fears as she was signing them in, taking their information, answering their questions, and making sure they were well taken care of. In other words, she had no time to be dealing with the snake. I remember being very reluctant at the thought of reaching down and somehow subduing the poisonous creature even though I knew I had to take charge of the situation. Luckily, life had taught me how to push my fear aside, and I was able to take control of the snake, grabbing it by the tail and pinching off its head and mouth so it couldn't strike.

I immediately walked over to Annette asking her what she wanted me to do with the snake. Somehow I knew these were her students and the lesson was hers to conduct. She told me to toss the snake onto the floor, which I promptly and gladly did, at which point Annette then took a shovel and nudged the snake outdoors where I assumed she disposed of its poisonous behavior by killing it. Normally, I would feel bad about killing a creature simply because it was exhibiting its natural instincts, but the snake in this dream was a very nasty and unruly creature and I was glad to see it go. After awakening from the dream, I immediately texted Annette to tell her about it, thinking she would find it amusingly odd. However, what we were both about to profoundly realize was that this dream was more a reality than either one of us ever considered.

When Annette received my text she didn't hesitate in calling me nearly out of breath with wonder and confusion saying, "You are never going to believe this!" Curiously, I wondered what the correlation could be, and then Annette began to tell me a very fascinating story. It seems she had been sick with a nasty cold for a couple of weeks that just wouldn't go away. But being a business owner, wife, and mother of a two-and-half-year-old, she certainly didn't have time to put her own needs first. Then one day, Annette and Rain were leaving the shop after a particularly busy day when Rain looked up at her mother and said, "Mommy, you have a snake around your neck." I was stunned. Annette said she didn't know what to think of it then, but now considering the dream I'd just had she was sure Rain was trying to help her get rid of whatever poisonous situation was creating her ill health.

Rain was already psychically clued into what Annette and I were just starting to realize. Consequently, Annette and I promptly discussed the symbolism of the dream and how the snake was the representation of the illness she currently needed to heal. It seemed that Annette had been experiencing some difficulty at work with clients who were not honoring her time and who were expecting her to take care of their irrational needs. The snake was the representation of the poisonous energetic nature of these people and their effect upon Annette's good nature. The way Annette was going to heal her cold was by putting her own needs first, and letting others take care of themselves. Once Annette finally understood what was creating her illness, she was then able to take the necessary steps to heal the situation and herself by learning to hold bigger boundaries with the people in her life who were not honoring her time and efforts. Before long, the snake was gone and Annette was back to full health, but I couldn't help but wonder what would have become of the snake and Annette's illness had Rain not provided us with the crucial added insight telling us that something bigger was going on. This just demonstrates the power of the next generation and their ability to see from a higher dimensional reality. Rain never once thought to question her outward reality even though it was a reality her mother and I could only see inwardly.

Only when we understand the reality of these quantum children can we actually foster their "superhuman" abilities properly. I personally believe that our current school systems are experiencing crises because the climate of change requires that we update our understandings about the quantum realities and what it now means to be educated today. The future is going to be a crazy place. If you thought it was difficult to get used to those new-fangled computer things, just imagine how hard it is going to be to keep up with the quantum technologies of the future. Still, everything has to start somewhere, and every person can begin to access the magic of the universe by first learning to listen to his or her own unique inner wisdom. The first task to listening to your inner wisdom is to give yourself permission to explore.

The Energetic Climate of Permission

The first step we as individuals must make toward our magical future is to give ourselves permission to know and permission to explore. However, permission can be a difficult thing for a lot of people. Most of us were raised with the ideal that permission is something we ask for from others, but not something we command for ourselves. While it's true that at times we need to seek the permission of others, at times we also need to give ourselves permission for the things we desire.

My father gave himself this type of permission when he taught himself to play the guitar. As a young man he had a strong desire to play in a bluegrass band, and so every day he would practice picking and strumming. Before long he grew to become an accomplished musician. However, my father's success didn't come simply because he practiced every day; his success never would have come he if hadn't first given himself permission to follow his desire.

The best way to begin practicing this shift toward self-permission is to claim time to sit quietly, close your eyes, and explore your inner reality. The following exercise is designed to do just that and will give you a specific point on which to focus inwardly as you begin to develop your inner wisdom and insight in the process of discerning the truth of your life.

Technique:
Renewable Sourcing

In this exercise, you will be learning the basic energetic foundation upon which you can further explore your inner reality. Later in this section we will discuss the entire quantum field, but for now, learning to renew your energy and set a new foundation is the beginning of your quantum exploration. During this exercise, you are encouraged to give yourself permission to experience the beauty that is inside you. Remember that there is no wrong way of doing this exercise, and even feeling or seeing nothing is something.

The purpose of this exercise is threefold. First, it is meant to give you a specific element within your energetic environment on which to focus. Second, it is meant to get you used to going inward and seeking your own answers. Third, it is meant to provide you with the necessary practice for developing your clairvoyant faculties. Like anything, your personal inner energy field needs to be renewed and recycled if you wish to maintain enough energy to sustain your way of being.

As you begin to explore inwardly and take charge of your personal energetic climates, you have to understand the basic mechanics of keeping your energy in a state of flow. These basic mechanics are grounding, releasing, and filling in.

Grounding is probably the single-most important tool. Grounding is an energetic idea that conveys to your spirit and your body that you are connected to the earth and are manifesting in this reality. In a lot of ways, grounding—via the use of a grounding cord that connects to your hips and runs down into the earth and connects to her core—serves as the anchor that tells the universe where you are docked and manifesting physically, emotionally, mentally, and spiritually.

If you are ungrounded when working with your body, you will be unable to amass enough density to bring your desires to fruition. If you are ungrounded in spirit, you will be unable to determine your best courses of action.

The grounding cord also serves as a release mechanism. Releasing is another point of permission that many of us don't claim for ourselves. Most of us feel we have to keep an eye on everything at all times. We often carry all our desires and concerns about family, career, love, etc., inside our individual energetic fields, never feeling as though we can step away from our responsibilities or desires. Releasing your worries and expectations down your grounding cord allows you the opportunity to clear your perspective and see things anew. Release by watching the energy flow out of your field, into your grounding cord, and down into the earth, reaching her molten core where it can be burned away and renewed.

Once you are grounded and have released, the next and final step is filling in. For this point of focus, we will be recognizing the sun as a symbol of life-giving and renewing energy. The sun is a renewable source that will transmute your energy back to its pristine and whole state. This sun will fill you up from head to toe, renewing and refreshing you like a radiant star.

FOCUS POINT:
GROUNDING

1. Take a moment to close your eyes and image you have a grounding cord from your hips all the way down to the center of the earth. Make that cord as wide as your hips. Notice that you can make this cord out of any material you desire. For instance, you might use a ribbon as a cord, or perhaps an oak tree or a large quartz crystal.

2. Take time to play with your grounding cord and try several different types of cords. Purposely release your old grounding and simply drop something new. Notice that you can cut off a cord and create a new one at any moment.

3. Remove your grounding cord all together and notice how you feel when you are ungrounded versus being connected. Then drop a new cord that allows you to feel safe, comfortable, and supported.

FOCUS POINT:
RELEASING

1. After grounding, notice that you have a field of space an arm's length out around you. Ask that all the energy within that field be released, sending it down your grounding cord and into the earth where it will be transmuted, or recycled.

2. Once you have emptied out your space, take a look around and notice if there is anything or anyone hanging around that doesn't want to leave. Maybe it's your child, or maybe it's a project from work, or it may even be your grandmother who has been

gone for twenty years. The point is to notice who or what is hanging out in your space and then give yourself permission to release the energy.

3. Once you know who and what is lingering in your space, go ahead and give yourself permission to fully release them from your field. This gesture of claiming your space is meant to remind you that you are an individual who must claim sovereignty in order to properly give to others. Remember that whatever you release will re-establish the minute you think of it again, but the point is that you can claim time and space for yourself first and foremost.

FOCUS POINT:
FILLING IN

1. After grounding and releasing, envision a large golden sun over the top of your head.

2. Ask to have all the energy that you released to come back to you through the sun. Watch as the energy you released into the earth filters upward into the sun above your head. Watch as the energy churns, recycling itself in the sun's energy.

3. Next, ask that any energy that you have left in other places, like home, work, or even the grocery store come back to you; watch as these energies make their way back to you, filtering into your sun, growing and expanding it.

4. Once all your energy has been called back, imagine reaching up and popping the sun like a balloon and watch as the energy of the sun fills up your space and permeates ever fiber of your being from head to toe.

Now that you understand how to ground, release, and fill yourself in, you can practice this many times a day. Whether you are at work, home, or even in the car, you can intend to ground, release your energy, and fill in your personal energy field with a golden sun. There will be times when you will want to do this process methodically, taking your time to watch as your cord connects, paying attention to the energy you are releasing, and allowing the sun to slowly fill you in; other times, you might want to quickly renew yourself by simply bringing your intent to grounding, releasing, and filling in. The point is to be conscious of renewing your energy several times a day.

2

You Are a Spirit in a Body

I once worked as a barista in a coffeehouse as a second job. As a clairvoyant, I was in the process of establishing my clientele and still needed another source of income. To be honest, during this period of time I was in a tremendous amount of resistance to the fact that I had to have a second job. I had practiced the laws of attraction for years, but was still having a hard time meeting my own needs. I was resentful for the fact that following my heart meant I would have to work twice as hard just to meet my basic needs. All I really wanted was to work at what I loved, which was being a clairvoyant. Yet how many of us actually get to work at what we love? I knew on some level I was being unrealistic, because the fact was that regardless of what was going on in the universe, I still needed to earn a living. Yet to be sure, the universe has an odd way of bringing to light what we need to understand in order to overcome our limitations. For me, that came in the form of a peculiar series of events at my second job.

The coffeehouse was allegedly haunted. It was located in an old house originally built in the late 1800s. The house had seen many families and businesses come and go. Over the years a lot of paranormal sightings had also been reported on the premises. Even the coffeehouse owner had reported seeing a small girl in the upstairs attic, and it was reported by many employees that they felt the presence of a man in the basement storage room. I, for one, saw an old woman once in the basement, but she wasn't attached to the house—she was the owner's mother who had been deceased for years. Yet for me, being a clairvoyant medium and seeing spirits is not unusual, in fact it is common. But one day I would encounter an unrelenting presence at the shop that was anything but common.

Coffeehouse hours begin prior to sunrise. It was never particularly fun to wake up at 4:30 in the morning just as I was experiencing my deepest dream state. Nonetheless, business needed to be conducted and my employer was counting on me to open the shop. The only thing that made it all worthwhile, because the money certainly didn't, was the clarity of the undisturbed dawn. There is something about that time of day that is magical. There is a tranquility that arises as the city sleeps and clarity is at its peak, allowing contemplation and meditation to be more powerful in the quiet and stillness of the otherwise-rushing energies.

That morning was like all others. It was summertime, and the cool morning air was crisp and refreshing, providing a nice contrast to the heat of the day. Despite my resistance, I felt invigorated and was eager to brew the first pot of coffee as I knew it would be my only opportunity to enjoy a hot pick-me-up all day. When I arrived at the shop, I was greeted by my fellow employee, Jack, who was in charge of the kitchen. We walked into the shop and immediately went up to the front counter to clock in on the register. When I flipped on the light switch, to my surprise I saw the figure of a man standing in the lobby. I jumped, startled with fear, but as quickly as he was there, he was gone.

I turned to Jack and said, "Did you see that?"

"Did I see what?" said Jack. It seemed there was no one there. I wondered if my eyes were playing tricks on me, or if perhaps I had just seen a ghost. Nevertheless, I wasn't there to act as a clairvoyant; I was there to be a diligent employee. I put the event out of my mind and went about my business.

I immediately began brewing the first pot of coffee. As I waited for it to finish, I hustled about assembling the espresso machine and preparing the register for the day. When the coffee was finished, I quickly ushered it out to the lobby and anxiously turned to grab a cup for myself. As I spun around, standing right in front of me was the same figure I'd seen when I turned on the lights. If I hadn't stopped dead in my tracks I would have walked right through him. But as quickly as I froze in fear, he dissipated before my eyes and was gone. My heart was racing and I didn't know what to do. Was someone trying to get my attention? If so, he wasn't sticking around long enough for me to find out what he needed.

His invasive behavior would persist all morning. As I went about my business, turning on the lights throughout the shop, and he would be there watching me. I would be stocking the mini-fridge, and he would be standing behind me looking over my shoulder. As comfortable as I am with otherworldly energies, this man was making me feel anxious and nervous, like I was exposed and vulnerable. As a spirit of any kind, he was blatantly overstepping his boundaries. Yet because I was working at my second job, I didn't think I had the time to sit and clairvoyantly deal with the situation energetically. Again, I was resentful that I couldn't do the job I needed to do, which was to help this spirit in obvious need of attention. Instead, I had a coffee shop to open.

At one point, after having been startled one too many times by the translucent man, I spoke out loud saying, "If you need my attention, this isn't the time. Check back in with me during my office hours." I conde-scendingly joked. I knew if I was forceful enough in my tone he would understand that I meant business. In my experience as a clairvoyant me-dium, spirits will conform to the authority we carry. It's just like what "dog whisperer" Cesar Millan says about owners taking authority and being the alpha dog. If we think we are powerless against spirits, then spirits can overpower us; however, if we hold our power and set the ground rules with spirits, then spirits will honor our authority. It seemed my tactic had worked and before long the shop was opened, business was booming, and the translucent man was nowhere in sight. I quickly forgot about his per-sistent need for attention. In fact, I would never have thought about him again if it hadn't been for the strange young man who entered the shop striking in me the same odd chord as the translucent figure.

An hour into the morning, a young man came into the shop. He was disoriented, jittery, and incoherent. His eyes were bugged out and wild. He reminded me of a character I had seen in a movie about meth addiction. I was helping another customer and the young man was pac-ing behind him impatiently, wanting my attention. His jitteriness was intrusive and he was making the other customers uncomfortable. When I finally and reluctantly got to him, he must have known that he was act-ing unusually because he kept apologizing for his strange behavior. He said, "I don't mean to freak you out, I just need to get something to eat but I don't have enough money." *Who does,* I thought. After all, that's why I was working two jobs, right? My resistance kicked in and rather than being sympathetic, I was a little resentful. His jitteriness and pacing told me he obviously had money for drugs and was now looking for a hand-out in meeting his basic needs.

I explained to the young man that I did not have the authority to give out free food, and that I couldn't help him with his problem. I hoped he would go away but instead he persisted, saying, "I'm just kind of nervous because I've had a lot of coffee today and I really need some food. Do you think you can make me a sandwich?" Just then, Jack walked by and I motioned for him to come and help me with this situation. Jack seemed to have a better rapport with young man and went to sit down with him to see if he could get his story. But as it turned out, my clairvoyance would kick in and I would become conscious of why this man was in need of help and how my helping him was also helping myself.

As I watched Jack sitting with the man, I was struck with the fact that this young man was making me feel just as uncomfortable as the translucent figure from earlier. I wondered what the connection between the spirit and man was all about. What was the connection between the spirit and the man? Was the translucent figure a passed-over spirit? Did he have something to communicate to this man? I stepped into the back room a moment and quieted my mind and asked for clarification on what I needed to know and do, if anything, about this situation. I expected the translucent figure to show up and tell me that he was the former drug-addicted friend of the young man and wanted to tell him to quit before it killed him, too. But the answer I received was far more profound than I could have conceived.

As I clairvoyantly viewed the event, I saw the translucent figure trying to sit on the young man's lap, except the man wouldn't sit still long enough for the spirit to rest in place. That's when I realized what was going on. The translucent figure was the spirit of the man himself. As I mentioned earlier, part of humanity's evolution into higher being requires a deeper understanding that we are both body and spirit, and that these two things working in cooperation ultimately allows us to experience heaven on earth. But based on the behavior of the young man, he was experiencing anything but heaven right now. His spirit and body were detached, and he was living in his own private hell. He was hungry, disoriented, and vulnerable.

Somehow, this young man's body and spirit had become severely separated. In that sense, the young man was what I would refer to as completely "out of body," causing his body and spirit to detach from one another. Just then, Jack came back and explained that the man had come to the coffeehouse earlier that morning for breakfast but we weren't open yet and so he went to another coffee shop but they didn't serve food. Not having anywhere to go, the young man had to purchase a coffee at the other shop until we were open and he could get a sandwich. Unfortunately, purchasing the coffee left him short on cash and now he didn't have enough money to buy a sandwich for himself.

I was suddenly aware of exactly what was going on. This young man was out of his body and his spirit had been hanging out in the one place it knew it could receive the help it needed in order to get back into its body. When I realized what was going on, I let go of my resistance to helping him and immediately went into the kitchen and made the young man a sandwich. Food is one of the best ways to either get back into the body or to simply stay in the body, which is why so many of us have weight issues; we are unconsciously trying to stay in our bodies. Perhaps if we could all become conscious of our spirits' needs and our bodies' needs then we wouldn't need to use food as an unconscious substitute. Still, I was taken aback by the severity of the young man's detachment. No matter what the cause of the separation, I knew it couldn't be healthy for either his spirit or his body. I never saw the young man again, but his message obviously sticks with me today.

When we have given ourselves permission to explore our inner wisdom, we first learn that we are more than just our bodies, we are spirits too. It's important to know the distinction between these two parts of ourselves, as part of our energetic climate change means learning to live by the magical and universal power of our spirits. It is through our spirits that we learn a higher way of living. The problem is that most of us are either unaware that we have a spirit, or we discount our spirit's ability. Inner wisdom tells us that we are spirits first who have created our bodies to enact within. If we don't know our spirit, we cannot know what we are enacting.

Are You Conscious of Your Spirit and Body?

The young man was clearly unconscious of the fact that his spirit was operating completely independently of his body. He was unconscious to the fact that his spirit was so powerful that it was already where his body wanted to be. The severity of his unconsciousness concerned me. The way in which I had been seeing his form all morning was different somehow. His spirit carried a lot of form, more than just a whiff of smoke or a flash of light; it had shape, density, and substance. When a spirit is that detached from the body, suddenly the body is without its guidance system, leaving it extremely vulnerable. That's what concerned me most. That type of vulnerability leaves the body unable to discern what is in its best interest, and can inadvertently allow destructive forces to channel through our behaviors. Have you ever wondered why we have ghosts, poltergeists, and possessions? It is largely due to being unconscious as to where our spirits reside. It also makes me wonder just how many "ghost" or "spirit" sightings are actually just unconscious people out of their bodies. When we unconsciously leave the body, we attract all kinds of curious beings, not all of them quite so nice or well intended. When we leave the body, we need to be protected and aware of what we are seeking so we are not overcome by what is lurking. Unfortunately, our social beliefs that drugs and alcohol are recreational greatly undervalue the power of these expansive substances. In truth, there is a sacredness and purpose to altered states. What that young man needed more than a sandwich was a shaman. However, you don't have to be high to be out of body. We all operate out of our bodies to some degree simply because we are mostly unaware of our spirits.

When the spirit is operating in the body, manifestation is the result, which is the benefit to being conscious of both our spirits and our bodies.

The spirit serves as the inspiration and the body serves as the vessel. We cannot conceive if we are unaware of our spirits, and we cannot manifest if we are out of our bodies. If the spirit and the body are not working together, then we have little or no control over our free will; therefore we are powerless to change our circumstances. The trick, then, becomes being able to keep track of our spirits and our bodies at the same time.

Take a moment to check in with yourself. Do you know where you are at this moment? Where is your body? Is it at home, or at the park, or in a lunchroom cafeteria? Where is your mind? It is at the office, or with the kids, or perhaps it is focused on reading? What about your spirit? What is your spirit experiencing at this moment? Is it joyful and uplifted, or is it doubting and uncertain, or maybe your spirit is simply curious and hungry for inner knowledge? Wherever you are, recognize that you can exist in many places at the same time. Your body can be at home while your mind is at work, yet you might be existing in both places at once. The fact is that we are spirits, we are bodies, and we have to honor all parts of ourselves if we want to have any effect over our free-will choices and how we operate.

Ultimately, when we speak of energetic climate change, it is the idea that we are ascending out of our unconsciousness and into our higher position of consciousness, thereby freeing ourselves from being ignorant of our spirits. Today is the day of recognizing that we are more than just our bodies—we are spirits too. By being conscious of our spirits, we save ourselves from our lower ways of being.

The Energetic Climate of Resistance

On the day I encountered the translucent figure at the shop, I was particularly in a state of resistance. I felt like I was living to fulfill only my physical needs at the expense of my spiritual needs. But I didn't just learn the importance of being conscious of my spirit on that day—I also learned that clairvoyance wasn't "work," but a way of life.

When I was in clairvoyance school, my teachers always said, "What you resist persists, and what you hold dear draws near." Resistance simply implies that you are unaware of what you are learning through your experiences. This is where taking charge of your energetic environment clues you in to the lessons you are learning so you can move out of resistance and into acceptance. I was resistant to the idea that I could be a clairvoyant unless I was on office hours. Thankfully, the persistent young man helped by reminding me that I could use my clairvoyant abilities at all times in my life, not just as a form of work. This information allowed my body and spirit to reconcile their needs by giving my spirit permission to shine in all my experiences. Suddenly I wasn't holding my spirit back because I wasn't where I wanted to be. Instead I was bringing my spirit into all that I did.

Technique:
Creating Earth and Universal Spirit Energy

Taking charge of your energetic environment means first understanding how it operates. As you have already learned to ground, release, and fill in, now you will be exploring the two currents by which all humanity operates. In this exercise, you will be inwardly focusing on the two elements of earth and universal spirit energy. These forces represent etheric currents of energy that you will run through specific channels in your legs and in through the brain and down the spine. The purpose of this exercise is to become familiar with the two basic human life energetic currents. In a later exercise, you will learn how to specifically work with these currents to generate your personal quantum field. For now this process is designed to help you release any resistance you might have about using your intuitive abilities.

FOCUS POINT:
GROUND, RELEASE, FILL IN

1. To begin this exercise, first ground, release, and fill yourself in with a radiant golden sun. It's always important to ground yourself before working with your energy just like you would if you were rewiring your home. Once you are grounded, you can begin to work with your earth and spirit energies.

FOCUS POINT:
EARTH ENERGY

1. Close your eyes and focus inward, placing your attention on your feet.

2. Ask to have a current of earth energy fill up your feet. Inwardly sense, using your intuition, the color and vibration of your earth energy. Remember there is no wrong way of doing this and all colors are correct. Just allow whatever color is right to present itself, noticing the texture and quality of the energy as it swirls in your feet.

3. Next, bring that stream of earth energy up through the legs following the bone. Bring the earth energy in through the shins, up past the knees, in through the thighs, up to the hips, around back to meet at the tail bone, and send the current down your grounding cord. This grounds out the flow and creates a loop, or natural cycle, that flows in from the earth, up through your legs, and then connects back to the earth.

4. Take a moment to notice how the earth energy is flowing. Follow the flow through the leg channels, checking for any obstacles or obstructions along the

way. There is no need to react to anything that you see. The point is just to become familiar with the energy current and the channel. Later, when you have gained more certainty about what you are seeing, you can change or correct anything you desire.

Focus Point:
Universal Spirit Energy

1. While still grounded and focused inward, place your attention on your crown, or "halo."

2. Call in your universal spirit energy from anywhere in the universe. You can bring it in from anywhere out in the universe, such as a planet, a constellation, or any place where you have felt happy and knowledgeable before; sense the color, quality, and texture of this energy.

3. Next, ask to have your spirit energy come in through the top of your head. Filling up the halo, let the spirit energy filter down through the top of the head, allowing the energy to follow along down the spine, splitting at the shoulders, and making its way down the arms and into the hands. Fill up your hands with spirit energy. Then allow the stream of energy to make its way back up the arms to the shoulder blades, allowing the flow to continue downward along the spine, all the way to the tail bone where it meets your grounding cord. Send your spirit energy down the grounding cord to be grounded out just like your earth current.

Your earth and spirit energy will not always stay the same color. As a matter of fact, you can intend certain colors and vibrations to come in and find your favorites. The point is that you understand you cannot create if you do not have earth energy running, and you cannot conceive new ideas if you don't have your spirit energy running. Practice running these energies several times a day and play with different colors and forms. Sometimes, if I need to feel passion for my creations, I will pull volcano energy into my earth channels. If I am in need of rest, I will pull the waters of Cayman into the earth channels. Other times, if I need a spark of creativity, I will pull the energies from the Gemini constellation into my spirit channels. Or, if I just need a little peace of mind, I pull a radiant yellow energy into my spirit channels, which sooths my soul. Play with your energy currents and find what you like best.

3

You Operate
in a Quantum
Field

Lola and I had been friends for years. Although we had been there for one another through many of life's ups and downs, Lola would face a tragedy that would flip her world upside down and she would never really be the same again.

Lola had been dating a wonderful man; Troy seemed right for her in every way. They enjoyed the same food, music, entertainment, and art. Art was something the two specifically had in common. Troy was a prolific artist whose paintings were hung in every home of everyone he ever knew. Lola loved this about him, as she truly appreciated the extent of his artistry. She anxiously waited for the day when she would receive a piece of artwork from him. Unfortunately, time was not on their side. Troy was suddenly struck with cancer, and within two months he was gone. Lola was devastated, and in the ensuing aftermath all of Troy's artwork was taken and put away by the family. Lola was hit with the fact that not only was her love gone, but she would never have one of his paintings by which to remember him. She felt as if there was a hole in her heart that would never be filled because she would never have a painting.

One day, while Lola was at work, a young woman walked in carrying what looked like a canvas wrapped in Christmas paper. The girl looked at Lola and said she had a gift for her. The woman was embarrassed as she handed it over. She said, "I know you don't know me, but I painted something for you." Lola didn't know what to make of it, but as she opened the gift, the young artist explained. It seemed that prior to Troy's passing he had encouraged the girl to pursue her artistic nature. Thanks to his promptings, she was now hanging her art in many venues and was beginning to sell some pieces. Yet as wonderful as life was going for the young artist, she couldn't help but think of the grief that Lola must be feeling during the holiday. In honor of Troy's passing and in honor of their love for one another, the young woman painted a picture in their memory. The young woman stood there awkward and uncertain as to whether her gift would be well received, after all, Lola new nothing of her and she knew nothing of Lola. However, little did the artist know that she was fulfilling Lola's greatest wish by bringing her the one thing that could fill her heart.

Some might call this story a random act of kindness but randomness is simply the universe bringing us that which we cannot conceive how to orchestrate for ourselves. We all operate in the same energetic stew, otherwise known as the quantum field. Quantum science is now verifying that all of us are energetically connected together in a coalescent field of energy in which our thoughts affect one another. Lola's thoughts were of wanting a painting, and her thoughts were received via telepathic magnetics by the young artist whose thoughts were of Lola and her time of grief. I personally think Troy was serving as the bridge between the two thoughts, whispering to the artist to give her a gift.

The Quantum Science of Universal Magic

There is universal magic that takes place when we hold a thought regarding what we wish to experience in our realities. The magic occurs when the thought vibration leaps into the field, telepathically reaching those in alignment with our intentions, and we are drawn together by magnetic common ground. Today's energetic climate change calls for us to recognize our quantum entanglement as part of our ascension into quantum beings. Yet how does this quantum reality work? How do our thoughts, individually and collectively, operate? Consciousness researcher Lynne McTaggart sums it up nicely in her epilogue to *The Field: The Quest for the Secret Force of the Universe*, "The Coming Revolution":

> *Discoveries are being made that prove what religion has always espoused: human beings are far more extraordinary than an assemblage of flesh and bones. At its most fundamental, this new science answers questions that have perplexed scientists for hundreds of years. At its most profound this is a science of the miraculous ... these studies offer us copious information about the central organizing force governing our bodies and the rest of the cosmos ... we are not a chemical reaction, but an energetic charge. Human beings and all living things are a coalescence of energy in a field of energy connected to every other thing in the world. ... We are attached and engaged, indivisible from our world and our only fundamental truth is our relationship with it.*

McTaggart is a leading researcher in the field of consciousness and its quantum effects. In her book, she speaks of a revolution that will come—the revolution of consciousness. It poses the idea that revolution doesn't come by war, but rather revolution comes through higher understanding. Quantum science is that higher understanding, and it is the science that can help us understand our relationship to our body and our spirit. It is the science that allows us to create new circumstances at any moment.

The problem facing all of us today is that we are conditioned to believe that life happens to us, and that we are the victims of circumstance. If we were merely a chemical reaction, this concept would make sense; if we were not creating the action, then we would simply be subject to the action. This antiquated type of thinking implies that we are nothing more than a consequence of something outside of ourselves. When we live as a consequence, life seems random and chaotic without design or purpose. We are now learning that we are not merely a chemical reaction; rather, we are a pure energetic charge. This fundamental shift in understanding changes everything. It suggests that perhaps we have more control over our realities than previously realized.

Using Conscious Intention

Quantum science has already proven that reality is driven by human thought and choice, or rather, intent. Hardy's Paradox states, "In a quantum state, photons that are observed change their attributes; for intention is the observation to create change. Without intent, nothing happens." Intent is the thought and choice that moves the field. A good example of the quantum energetic principle of observation and intent can also be found in Dr. Masaru Emoto's conscious experiments with water. Emoto studied the way water's crystalline structures changed simply due to the intentions being held by the person observing the water. Intentions such as love and peace created beautifully complex geometric structures, something like snowflakes, while intentions such as hate and fear created grotesque and ill-formed structures more like blobs and unhealthy masses. This suggests that we, being mostly water, are what we intend.

The most powerful quantum part of the human DNA is its capacity to set intentions. The most important factor of intention is the spirit in which it was conceived. There are lower intentions and higher intentions. Some intentions hold a lower vibration in which the intention only serves to perpetuate the belief in separation, or "every man for himself," while other intentions are higher vibrations that not only serve the individual but serve another or the greater whole. For instance, when you receive a gift from someone, the gift itself doesn't matter so much as the spirit in which the gift was given. Your Aunt Tilley might send you the same pair of fuzzy slippers every year at Christmastime, and although you never wear them, you graciously accept them because you understand that they were given in the spirit of love and appreciation. Unfortunately, not all intentions are honorable. Imagine working for a corporation like Enron (or any corporation or organization that has committed fraud against its employees and customers). The corporation's intentions toward its employees and customers would be to hoard and withhold gains from the very people generating the flow of profits. Suddenly, the gift of a job or the wonder of a product isn't really wonderful given the spirit of intent.

The key difference between these two intentions is that the lower intention leads to submission and domination, while higher intention leads to acceptance and cooperation. When we know the intention, we can calculate the outcome. If the intention is for good, the result will be wonderful; subsequently, if the intention is for ill will, the result will be disaster. One of the best ways to gauge the spirit of someone's intent is to first become familiar with your own.

Take some time every day to ask yourself, *What are the intentions behind my communications? What are the intentions of my actions? What are the intentions of my desires?* If you are using your communications to gain control over another person, the intent will backfire, creating an effect you didn't really want. If you are communicating with the best interest of all parties involved, your intent will see great results. The same can be said for our actions and desires. If the intentions behind our actions and desires are of a lower vibration, they will result in lower vibrating experiences, such as separation and disharmony. However, if your actions and desires are of a higher vibration, they will create higher experiences, such as connection and elation. Every individual is responsible for their intentions and how those intentions flow through the quantum field. It's time for us all to get to know what we are personally contributing and decide if it is in our own best interest, and whether or not it serves the greatest good. We must then resolve to change any intention that does not hold a higher vibration.

There is a bonus to gauging our own intentions. When we are conscious of our personal intentions, we suddenly have more knowingness about the intentions of others, making us less susceptible to manipulation and foreign control. The key to mastering the power of intent is not about trusting other people; rather, mastering intent means knowing the truth of our motivations and then realizing that those motivations will magnetize like-minded people and events.

The Energetic Climate of Effort versus Effortlessness

A thought is a simple thing. It takes no effort to have a thought. The stronger the thought, the more magnetizing power it has to manifest itself in the physical. Some thoughts are so powerful they seem like miracles but in reality all thoughts are miraculous. Many people think all you ever have to do is maintain positive thinking and life will unfold beautifully around you exactly as you expect it without doing anything to make it happen. However, what I have experienced living as the eternal optimist is that if you don't take an action toward your desires they can never come true.

Both inaction and action are necessary for propelling energy. If you just sat at home thinking of winning the lottery and took no action toward achieving your goal, your chances are almost zero that you will manifest your desire. On the other hand, if you buy a ticket your chances automatically increase, and not just because you purchased a ticket, but because you took an action in your physical reality in alignment with your desires. In other words, the universal law of magnetics mirrors your response to your desires and then matches it; therefore, if you do nothing, the magnetics do nothing. However, when you take an action toward your desires, no matter how small, you rev up the magnetics and build energy toward your creation. This is what it means to allow your spirit to embody your experiences. But don't be fooled into thinking that manifesting desires is all about taking action; there is much more to it than that.

I have a dear friend who one day said to me, "I am a human being and you are a human doing." Her point being that I tend to think that I alone have to solve all the problems of the world today. I was raised with the belief that "if you have time to lean, you have time to clean." However, that way of living doesn't provide much time for rest or relaxation so you can continue your non-stop pace. Not to mention, if we are always trying to do something to create our desires then we are not necessarily allowing the universe to bring to us the randomness we cannot conceive but which can be better then we could ever expect or imagine.

Magic is a fine art. The magnetics of inaction and action must be properly balanced between being and doing in order for your creations to manifest as you desire. All action has the same level of impact as no action. This is where energy is not an all-or-nothing thing. There is a time to rest and a time to work. The trick is to find your own internal rhythm. Being and doing must have balance in order to allot for proper inspiration and timing. Have you ever worked yourself to a frazzle only to accomplish nothing? Have you ever come home from a vacation feeling refreshed and invigorated ready to take all of life's challenges? There is a time to do and time to be. Given the magnetics of the shifting period of time we are in today, it is extremely helpful to know when is the ebb and when is the flow, and to honor when to do and when to be so we don't inadvertently take ourselves off course.

Technique:
Generating Your Quantum Field

If you are like me, and you have a hard time being and not doing, this next exercise will give you something to do while you are being. If you have a hard time doing and not being, this exercise will help you learn how to move your energy so you can get going. Once you balance your doing and being, you can monitor your field and take appropriate action or non-action when necessary, which is ultimately how you stay in what we call the "flow."

When you do this exercise, use your conscious intention to simply command the energies to do as you ask. You don't have to know if you are doing it right, because there is no right or wrong way of doing it. Just follow along, and over time you will gain an understanding of how it works for you. For now it's perfectly acceptable to feel awkward and uncertain about how you operate as a quantum being... it takes a little time. What is import is that you understand that you are in charge of directing the energies. Simply watch as they flow and create what is your field.

When you think about effort and effortlessness, allow this process to be effortless by simply allowing it and not second guessing what you are seeing or experiencing. Remember this isn't the time to do anything about what you are sensing; this time is for learning to observe and notice your field and the force of your intentions within it. This is a simple exercise, yet it represents the fundamental mechanics of your personal quantum field, and serves as the basis for the rest of your explorations. I suggest performing this exercise daily so you start getting familiar with the process.

FOCUS POINT:
GROUND, RELEASE, FILL IN

1. Begin by grounding, releasing your energy, and filling in your space.
2. Once you are grounded, you can begin to run your earth and spirit energies from the previous exercise.

FOCUS POINT:
MIXING EARTH AND UNIVERSAL ENERGY

1. Next, place your attention at the tail bone or base of the spine, noticing how your earth and spirit energies are running together.
2. Take a strand of earth and a strand of spirit and wind the two energies together. (It is suggested that you take 85 percent earth and 15 percent spirit. Mix it around and see what works best for you.)

FOCUS POINT:
CREATE YOUR FIELD

1. Concentrate on your breathing for a moment.
2. Take a deep breath and feel the earth and spirit energy move upward through the center of your body.
3. As you exhale, allow the energy to fall back down to the base of the spine.
4. With the next breath in, pull the energy further up through the body and then exhale down again.
5. Repeat your breathing, allowing the energy to climb higher with each breath until the energy stream reaches the top of your head.
6. With your next breath, allow the energy to come up and out of the head and fountain out around you, creating a bubble or field approximately an arm's length around you.

7. Simply sit in your field and notice how it feels to have your energies running and forming your personal magnetic field.

As I said before, practice running your energy and creating your field every day. You can reset your energy any time you wish by simply focusing and giving it a new direction. For example, if you want to run your energy with the focus of being calm, direct your earth current to begin pulling in a stream of energy that is soothing and relaxing. The point is to start acclimating to your energetic climate so you can take charge over maintaining it.

4

You Are in
Charge of
Your Field

One of the greatest lines in movie history has to be, "May the force be with you" from *Star Wars*. Yet, as so many of us playfully reiterate this phrase to one another, seldom do we actually believe there is such a thing as a force, and if we do believe in a force, we tend to think only certain "gifted" people have access it. Yet the force is really just our ability to intuit the intentions within the field and alter that which doesn't serve the greatest good. The real trick is in learning how to work with the force so that we can achieve the outcome we desire. Just like Luke Skywalker had to undergo the training of a master Jedi before he could be in charge of his own destiny, we too must learn to master our intuitive "Jedi-senses" before we can effectively work with the force to affect change within our field. Once we are capable of altering our fields, we can then begin to take charge of our destinies by creating new circumstances in our realities.

The force is always with us. We are the force. And the force is ours with which to create. Today's shifting climate requires that we all learn to manage and operate our own field. When we are in control of our individual fields, we are suddenly not-so-easily manipulated by seemingly unstoppable forces, and we understand how to alter our circumstances to achieve our desired outcomes. Yet, just like anything, learning to have control over our field means learning a new science—the science of the sixth sense, or that which is our higher intuitive perceptions and how they operate in conjunction with the field. The way to access the central organizing force that governs the coalescent field is through the use of our higher senses. Raising our energetic climate requires that we become adventurous by exploring the gifts these senses bring.

The Purpose of the Sixth Sense

Our educational system today only focuses on the science of the five senses: sight, touch, taste, sound, and smell. These senses are fixed and limited to the physical and tangible world. Yet, there is a sixth sense that belongs to our spirits and works in conjunction with the coalescent field that must be explored today. The sixth sense matches those of the five senses in that we have the ability to see, hear, touch, smell, and taste; however, with the sixth sense, instead of those sensations being outward experiences, they are inward sensations. Close your eyes and imagine biting into a lemon. What do you feel, sense, see, taste, and imagine? Those sensations are attached to your sixth-sensory perceptions. Although you are not in this moment eating a lemon, you are sensing the experience inwardly with your higher intuitive senses. Unlike the five senses, the sixth sense comprises many talents and latent abilities, including clairvoyance, imagination, telepathy, telekinesis, and teleportation, to name a few, and serves as the navigational tool that operates as our inner-guidance system for conceiving, maintaining, and assessing our relationship to the energies within the quantum field at any given moment.

The good news is that we don't have to go to school to learn how to use our intuitive abilities, although it certainly would be nice to have the option. In truth, the science of the sixth sense is a self-taught art, knowledge, and discipline. Symbolism is the art and language of the sixth sense that everyone must interpret for his or her self. What we interpret becomes our knowledge, and what we learn, we adapt as a new discipline and way of being. No longer can humanity afford to ignore this higher science, because it is the only thing that is going to bring us into sustainable balance.

Is Your Sixth Sense Working?

Whenever I tell a client that we are all clairvoyant, they look at me with dismay. They either do not believe or they do not realize that they have an innate sixth-sense faculty that can be of assistance to them in their lives. They think clairvoyant abilities are given only to a select few. However, as I have been teaching the tools of the sixth sense over the past several years, I have never found anyone who was not clairvoyant and who could not develop their sixth sense, as it is a fundamental part of our being.

We experience our sixth sense in many ways. I classify these abilities as clairvoyant, yet I could just as easily say "psychic abilities," as both incorporate much more than their labels imply. Clairvoyance is an individual sense, but I use it to classify all the senses that are housed under what is known as our *clair,* or "clear," abilities.

Clair abilities are the senses we use to retrieve and interpret sixth-sensory symbolism and information. The four categories of clair abilities consist of clairvoyance (clear seeing), clairaudience (clear hearing), clairsentience (clear sensing), and claircognizance (clear knowing). Clairvoyance enables us to see places, people, and objects within the mind's eye. Clairaudience allows us to hear the vibration and information from your soul or spirit guides, and can be sensed as voices, tones, bells, music, songs, or other types of sound. Clairsentience enables us to sense or feel emotions from other people, places, or things. Claircognizance facilitates our ability to simply know something to be true or untrue.

Here is an experiment you can try that will test your clair abilities to see if they are working: Close your eyes and imagine a rose, just like the flower, out in front of you and recognize that you can view this rose from all angles. This rose can be any color and shape and size that it wants to be, and all you have to do is notice what you notice about the rose. Take a minute and examine the rose. Notice the richness of its color and feel the texture of the petals. Listen to the hum and the vibration of your rose and sense how the rose feels to you emotionally. Follow the rose down and examine its stem. Move your fingers along the stalk, stopping where you might find leaves, thorns, or knots. Take a moment to contemplate how this rose looks, at the frequency of its vibration, the state of its emotions, and the spirit of its desire. Everyone will see their rose slightly differently. Some will envision a rose that is in full bloom, while others will envision a rose that is closed and still in the growing stages. The point is, everyone will see or feel something, at which point they are being clairvoyant and using their sixth sense.

Many times, people think this type of exercise is imaginary and don't believe that they are actually acting on clairvoyance. However, your imagination works with your intuitive faculties. Think of it like this … when you viewed your rose, you saw it as white. Why did you imagine that color versus any other? There are a myriad of colors that could have shown up, why that one? To one person, white might mean purity and to another, it might mean peace. Determine why your rose is speaking to you about where, when, why, and how to apply purity or peace in your life. Don't fear your imagination in this process; it helps form a picture of what your spirit is trying to convey. You just have to allow it and not force it to become something you think you need or want.

Ultimately, it doesn't matter what you see and find with this rose. Inward reality is just as "real" as outward reality. What matters is that you are viewing it using all of your sixth sensory perceptions. You can develop your sixth sense by taking this exercise a step farther and symbolically attaching the rose to yourself and assessing what the rose is saying about you in that moment. The bud could symbolize your spirit, and the stem could symbolize your body. Notice the condition of both your spirit and your body? Is the bud open or closed? What does the color tell you about how your spirit is feeling about its journey? The symbolism of color is different for every person. One person may interpret red as anger and another will interpret it as passion. Go with your gut instinct as to what you think the color or vibration of your rose means. Next, see if the stem is thick and healthy, or dried up and brittle. What does that stem say about your physical body and how it is dealing with the circumstances of your life? Notice whether the bud and the stem are working in tandem, or if your body and spirit are working apart. You may not get your answers right away, but rest assured you are developing the abilities that will lead you to your answers eventually.

The biggest value our sixth sense offers us is the ability to consciously change anything we see that we do not wish to create in our lives. For instance, if your bud was closed tightly and it did not want to open, you could take measures toward being diligent with your exploration of spirit and devoting time to meditation and contemplation so your bud could blossom. If your stem was brittle and withering, you could give the body more rest and start a new diet and exercise routine that would promote a healthier exterior. In other words, our clairvoyant faculties are our lifeline to health and happiness.

Through our spirits, we can tap into our clair abilities and determine what is truth and what is fiction. But more importantly, we can use our clair abilities to monitor our personal magnetics, ensuring that we are fully conscious at all times. These clair abilities allow us to perceive what is happening in the nonphysical (or quantum) realities, making them the "gift" that allows us access to the central organizing force that ultimately creates our lives.

Managing Your Field

Managing our higher senses begins by understanding the quantum nature of our fields. We all have a personal energetic field of which we are responsible for maintaining, as our field influences the collective field. Each individual has an operating system made up of a series of magnetic vortices called *chakras*. A chakra is a magnetic spinning wheel that creates something like a black hole that can draw in or send out light frequency energy, which in turn becomes a layer of our energetic fields or what many metaphysicians call the "aura," or rainbow light body, which is just another way of describing our personal quantum fields. Each person operates with seven major chakras that run up the spine and regulate the functions of the individual. For example, the third chakra (located mid-spine, below the rib cage) relates to the mental body's desire for power, the emotional body's need for self-respect and self-worth, and the spiritual body's ability to be courageous. It also regulates the physical body functions of the liver and the pancreas, just to name a few.

When I attended clairvoyant school, I learned to observe, or "read," chakras clairvoyantly. Within the chakras exist all the light frequency imprints of every experience we have ever had in this lifetime and in past lifetimes. Reading the chakras was really just about viewing the many pictures that had been imprinted within the multiple layers of a person's individual field. If these pictures were positive they were having a positive impact, and if the pictures were negative they were having a negative impact within a person's life. Of course the goal became to rectifying our negative imprints so we could experience more peace and joy.

The Energetic Climate—Inward and Outward

Think about this a moment: you are bigger on the inside then the outside. If you have ever watched Dr. Who, you know this is the concept of his telephone booth. From the outside it is a small, old-styled English phone booth, but when you step inside it's an expansive engine room and cockpit that drives his spaceship and propels him throughout the universe. The same is true for our spirits. Our spirits and their chakras may be housed in our bodies, but they are far more expansive than their vessels. When we look into the depths of our chakras and the aura they create, we see our greatest magic lies in our ability to affect our inward reality, as those effects eventually manifest in our outward circumstances.

The biggest revelation of our times today is that our inner reality creates our outward circumstances. Think about the implications of this statement. If our lives are outwardly chaotic, then we are inwardly in chaos, too. But what if you were to reconcile your inward chaos? What would that do to your outward life? It would have the same result. If you achieved inner peace, life around you would become peaceful. The reason the earth is in crisis is because her human stewards have forgotten that they are spirits; we have forgotten that we are bigger on the inside and have the magic of the universe at our disposal. The time is now to explore the inside of your personal telephone booth, find the magic that rests within your personal energetic field, and determine how you wish those energies to flow so that your inner reality matches what you wish to experience outwardly.

Technique:
Activating Your Chakras

In this exercise you will be building upon the fundamentals of the last few exercises. In a sense, this is where the foundation for exploring your spirit all comes together and the real journey begins. This exercise provides you with an expanded understanding of the chakras and their functions so you can begin acknowledging the types of energies they store. In this practice of running energy, the earth and spirit currents are directed upward through the body, opening the chakras until they fountain out from the crown above your head, forming your personal matrix. The practice of running energy is something I do daily, and even several times a day. The purpose is to pay attention to the field so you can know what you are creating in your life. I recommend that you run your energy daily, if not several times a day, until it feels like second nature.

FOCUS POINT:
GROUND, RUN EARTH AND SPIRIT ENERGY
1. Begin by grounding, releasing your energy, and filling in your space.
2. Once you are grounded, you can begin to run your earth and spirit energies from the previous exercise.

FOCUS POINT:
MIXING EARTH AND UNIVERSAL ENERGY
1. Next, place your attention at the tail bone or base of the spine noticing how your earth and spirit energies are running together.
2. Take a strand of earth and a strand of spirit and wind the two energies together.

FOCUS POINT: RUNNING ENERGY
UP THROUGH THE CHAKRAS CREATING OUR FIELD
1. With a deep breath, pull the earth and spirit energy up into the first chakra at the base of the spine. Allow the first chakra to spin and fluff up that layer of your aura, saying hello to your safety, security, home, and finances. Take a moment to notice the colors, vibrations, and sensations of the energies in

your chakra and contemplate whether or not it is in balance. If you don't like something you see in your field, release it down your grounding.

2. Next, breathe the earth and spirit energies up from the first chakra into the second, located in the pelvis. Spin the second and fluff up that layer of your field, saying hello to your creativity, passion, desire, sexuality, lower emotions, and inner wisdom. Take a moment to notice the colors, vibrations, and sensations of the energies in your chakra, and contemplate whether or not it is in balance. If you don't like something you see in your field, release it down your grounding.

3. Breathe the energy up from the second chakra into the third, just below the rib cage, and spin and fluff that layer of the aura, saying hello to your power, focus, will, and drive. Take a moment to notice the colors, vibrations, and sensations of the energies in your chakra, and contemplate whether or not it is in balance. If you don't like something you see in your field, release it down your grounding.

4. Breathe the earth and spirit energy up from the third chakra into the fourth, found in the heart. Open the heart chakra and expand that layer of the aura, acknowledging your ability to be compassionate and to love others as well as yourself. Take a moment to notice the colors, vibrations, and sensations of the energies in your chakra, and contemplate whether or not it is in balance. If you don't like something you see in your field, release it down your grounding.

5. Next, breathe up from the fourth chakra into the fifth, located in the throat. Spin your throat chakra and say hello to your communications, as well as your ability to express your emotions, speak the truth of yourself, and honor the truth of others. Take a moment to notice the colors, vibrations, and sensations of the energies in your chakra, and contemplate whether or not it is in balance. If you don't like something you see in your field, release it down your grounding.

6. Breathe the stream of earth and spirit energy up into your sixth chakra, or third eye chakra, found in the center of your head. Fluff up that layer, saying hello to your intuition and your inner self. Take a moment to notice the colors, vibrations, and sensations of the energies in your chakra, and contemplate whether or not it is in balance. If you don't like something you see in your field, release it down your grounding.

7. Lastly, breathe the earth and spirit energy up from your sixth chakra and into your seventh—the crown—found just above your head, or where the halo resides. As you pull that energy up, allow it to fountain out around you, creating the last layer of your auric field. Say hello to your connection to the Divine as well as your knowingness, personal authority, and outward face you put on for others. Take a moment to notice the colors, vibrations, and sensations of the energies in your chakra, and contemplate whether or not it is in balance. If you

don't like something you see in your field, release it down your grounding.

As you run your energy daily, notice the different colors, images, and sensations that you come across in each of the chakras. If you find something interesting, sit with it awhile and investigate its symbolism, and focus on what it tells you about what you've created in your life.

Technique:
Claiming Your Space

Once you have your energy running, you will want to protect the field you just generated. To do this, we use the universal symbol of a rose. One of the simplest tools I teach is that of the rose boundaries. This tool has immense power; many students have commented on how this gentle form of holding their boundaries aids them in not giving themselves away to others' demands. Many people have a difficult time holding their ground with others, of which the pending result is anger and resentment. Yet holding your boundaries doesn't have to be a harsh or angry endeavor, which is the true beauty behind using roses to create healthy boundaries.

The rose itself is a symbol of our ability to see ourselves in the reflection of other people. As you energetically place your roses around yourself, claiming your boundaries, you are gently sending out a signal that tells others what you wish or do not wish to experience. More importantly, you are also sending a signal that honors the people around you by also symbolically saying, *I honor others as I honor myself.* The greatest thing about this tool is that it can be used to hold boundaries for anything. For instance, if you would like to keep your office space or car protected from negative energies, you can put roses around those spaces to invoke the types of boundaries you desire.

Focus Point:
Creating Protection and Boundaries

1. After establishing your chakra field, imagine a giant rose, as big as yourself, out in front of you.

2. Take a moment to simply notice the rose. What color is the rose? Is it opened in full bloom, or closed in a tight bud? What does the stem look like? Does it have thorns and leaves? Simply notice its condition.

3. Next, tell the rose how you would like it to serve you. Communicate to your rose the types of experiences you desire, as well as what you do not desire.

4. Once you have given your rose boundary definition, duplicate the rose in front and in back, side to side, top to bottom, and all around, establishing your perimeter of roses, being sure to give yourself plenty of room within your bubble to operate.

5. Check in with your roses periodically throughout your day. If the roses are looking wilted or fatigued, simply toss them away and re-establish new boundaries.

Roses serve as boundaries and they also serve as hellos. What I mean is that if you are having a difficult time with a person, you can send them an energetic rose of compassion, acceptance, and cooperation. You will be surprised how someone acts differently to you even though they may not know what you are doing.

Technique:
Claiming Your Sovereignty

The last exercise in this series is meant to help you start claiming authority over your experiences. Claiming your sovereignty means drawing a clear understanding between your wisdom and the wisdom of others. The point being that we all have our own knowledge, truth, and wisdom, yet seldom do we rely on our own inner knowledge to provide us with the answers we are seeking. Think back on how many times you sought the advice of a friend because you didn't think you knew the best course of action for yourself. Claiming your sovereignty allows you to have a clear access to what is in your best interest and right for you personally.

Once you claim your autonomy, you can enter that sacred space whenever you need wisdom, understanding, or solace. The reason this space is exclusive to you is to allow you to become comfortable with and aware of your own energy away from and outside of everyone else's. This way when a foreign energy (energy that has been claimed by another person and is not yours) enters your field you will know instantly whether it is positive or negative and exactly what type of impact it will have on your experiences. This in turn allows you to determine your best course of action in relationship to the energy.

What does it mean to own the center of your head? First, the center of head can also be referred to as the third eye, or sixth chakra, and is the place where you seek your own inner wisdom. In that sense, your center of head is your point of authority and command over yourself and your circumstances. Therefore, it is also a space that is meant for only you. If you go into your center-of-head space and find someone else hanging out, such as your mother, or sister, or boss, you are encouraged to politely escort them out of your room. The reason for keeping this space strictly exclusive to yourself is so you can keep outside influences from taking precedence over your own intuitions.

I like to check in with my center of head by using this tool because it makes me feel empowered to be able to claim time and space just for myself. It is freeing to use this tool of clearing out your third eye after a particularly busy day of interacting with others.

Focus Point:
Building Your Room

1. Begin by closing your eyes and allowing yourself to breathe deeply, counting to six with the inhale, holding for a few seconds, then releasing with the exhale for a count of six.

2. Place your attention in your third eye (or sixth chakra).

3. Now begin to imagine a room in the center of your head. This room is exclusive to you … no one else will be in the room, nor are they to be given permission to be in the room. The point being, this area is meant to give you a place to go when you need to disconnect from everyone else and find your own insight and information.

4. Let your imagination begin to decorate your room. Give it the types of walls you desire, and bring in the furnishings and pictures that bring you comfort. I have added a massage table in my room so if I ever need self-healing, I can lie on the table and receive the healing I need. Allow yourself to decorate your room any way you want.

Focus Point:
Clean Out Your Center-of-Head Room

1. Sit quietly and close your eyes and enter your center-of-head room.

2. Stand in the doorway for a moment and survey your room. Take note of all the people you have brought with you in your mind. Notice if you brought your spouse, a friend, maybe even a coworker or two. You have allowed those others in the room to have sway over your life's circumstances.

3. Approach the people in your room, handing each a rose in recognition of their light. Ask them why they are claiming authority in your life. There is no need to engage them about their response while they are in your center-of-head room. Simply listen, and then gently guide them out.

4. If you are having a hard time asking someone to leave, like your favorite grandmother or best friend, because you know their intentions are loving and pure of heart, remind yourself that each person has the innate right to claim their own truth and knowledge outside of what anyone else teaches or implies. So even though you may love and appreciate the people who are showing up in your center-of-head room, give them a rose and politely let them know that you will meet up with them somewhere else, but that this space you now hold for yourself.

5. Once your room is clear of outside influence, set a rose boundary around your room to let everyone know that the space you hold in the center of your head is the place where you can seek your own authority as to what is best for your life.

Your room will serve as a bigger tool later when you get more into the reading and movement of energy. However, for now, keep this exercise simple. Decorate your room and spend lots of time in there feeling comfortable and relaxed, and get to know yourself again.

PART II

Evolving into Heaven on Earth

5

The Soul's Quest for Something Higher

It is said that meditation is the best way to seek inner wisdom. Yet for me, learning to meditate was difficult. I had an idea in my head that said meditation was strictly about being still and quieting the mind. Although I have since learned that while quieting the mind is absolutely beneficial to our well-being, meditation isn't just for blocking it all out; meditation can be interactive and explorative as well. The truth is, I'm a Gemini and you can't tell a Gemini not to think. My mind had only one speed (FAST!), and it was nearly impossible for me to simply be still. First of all, at the time in my life when I began meditating, I was still raising three young boys, which meant quiet times were precious and few. Not to mention we were on the go and active. I didn't have a lot of time to devote to doing what seemed like nothing. But I was at a point in my life where it was either do or die.

I recall rushing around one day, running from work to get the kids from school, so we could make it to hockey on time, and as always we were running late—not because we weren't prepared, but because we were simply trying to cram too much into the time we didn't actually have to begin with. On this day particularly, I recall driving in a rush and running a red light, knowing full well what I was doing. I knew the light was turning, and I floored it even though it was obviously too late. I swear it was only by the grace of God that we made it through the light and that my children were unharmed by my act of sheer desperation. Unfortunately, the same couldn't be said for my heart. I could feel it beating out of my chest with an overwhelming anxiety accompanied by a pain so intense I thought I was going to have a heart attack. That's when I knew the lifestyle I was living was killing me. If my soul had a purpose, it surely wasn't for the sake of living desperately just to meet some unrealistic goal. It's funny how life has a way of putting everything into perspective in an instant. In that moment, I became determined to master this thing called meditation in the hopes that it would lead me to a new way of living.

At the time I was learning to meditate, I was reading different books on metaphysics. One of my favorite books was called the *Edgar Cayce Companion: A Comprehensive Treatise of the Edgar Cayce Readings.* This comprehensive manuscript consisted of a compilation of Cayce's readings, channelings, teachings, and treatments. For a metaphysician like me, his book served as an all-encompassing reference to the bigger questions of life. It was in this book and another book on Cayce's work called *The Edgar Cayce Primer: Discovering the Path to Self-Transformation* that I came across his understanding of the soul and its purpose. Since I was looking for a new purpose to life, Cayce's insights seemed to be exactly what I was seeking. As Edgar Cayce is recognized as an authority on the workings of our spirits and souls, I figured his explanations would prove to be thought provoking at the very least. However, what it actually prompted was more than I ever expected; to say the least, it changed my entire perspective.

In *The Edgar Cayce Primer,* Cayce says, "The purpose of a soul is to be companions with God." In turn, the soul becomes the mean by which the Creator would come to know itself. Cayce explains that, "If God is love, then how could God express love other than through relationship?" In other words, the souls are the relationships God created in order to share Divine love. Cayce also said, "The soul, being Divine, participates in the most essential qualities of the Divine, which are the continuity of life and awareness. As co-creators with God, we are destined to participate in ever-growing, more meaningful, exciting creative expressions." In a sense, the soul would venture out and create in the name of the Creator, and through the soul's creative expressions the Creator would come to know itself. In other words, the soul's purpose is to perpetuate life and awareness.

Once the soul had ventured so far away from God that it no longer remembered the Creator, the soul would face its greatest quest—the journey back to the Creator. Then, and only then, would the soul be a true companion of God. The soul would know what it was with God and what it was without God, and it would come back with full perspective so the Creator would know its own totality. Cayce finished his discussion about the soul by saying, "As children of God, we are heirs to all the dimensions of the universe." After reading this, I was very intrigued about the idea of a dimensional universe, and so I decided that from now on I was going to use my meditation time as exploration time instead. I wanted to know what these dimensions were and why they were my rite. Thus began my inner exploration. I first asked the angels to keep me safe, and then I asked them to show me something I didn't know. At first, the explorations felt forced, like I was trying to make something happen; then, one day, I had a vision.

Seeing is Believing

One day while meditating and asking to go some place I had never been before, I had a sensation come over my body that was something like having a fever but not feeling sick. I felt as though the room had gotten larger while I had gotten smaller. It was then that I had a vision of myself as a large, translucent being standing over the earth looking upon it from a universal perspective. I had a very distinct feminine essence, and I sensed a golden crown above my head. It felt to me that this was a higher expression of myself, and that it was my honor and duty to serve as a guardian and steward to the earth. I noticed the earth was wrapped in something resembling a spider web, except that the web did not exist in the physical; it existed in a space of pure energy and information. This is where I realized that there were multiple planes of existence all experiencing the same moment. There seemed to be something like a point that represented the first dimension. There was a flat plane like a piece of paper that represented the second dimension. And then there were dimensions three, four, and five, which became the focus of my exploration although there were yet more dimensions beyond these.

I came to understand that the earth represented the third dimensional reality of matter and form, while the web exists in the fourth dimensional reality of light and information. All the while, I watched over the earth from my fifth dimensional reality, or higher self. I found that the third dimension is what we know to be our reality today. The third dimension is tangible and solid and can be measured as physical matter. The fourth dimension, however, exists as pure light and information. The fourth dimension isn't necessarily measureable because it doesn't exist as matter; instead, it operates as pure intent and possibility. The fifth dimension operates as an observation deck for our spirits where we can objectively view, via our clairvoyant abilities, the intentions of the fourth dimension and how they manifest into our third dimensional reality. This is when I understood that I had a physical self and a spiritual self, and that the space in between consisted of all the information necessary for creating the reality of my choosing, or what some might call heaven on earth.

As I continued my exploration from my fifth-dimensional higher self, I explored the fourth-dimensional webbing surrounding the earth plane in more detail, wondering what information needed to be pulled together in order to create my heaven on earth. I immediately noticed there were billions of points of light at each of the intersecting strands. I was struck with the thought that this mass intersecting-connectedness was much like the Internet in that we all have connection to one another through it. Each point of light represented an individual soul upon earth whose thoughts moved through the web like telepathy. It would seem that each soul knew what the other souls knew as they were all connected by their thoughts. As we know, thought creates reality, and so it must be that the soul's thoughts were responsible for creating their heaven on earth.

I zeroed in on one of the souls to see what they were thinking. What I saw was ball of light, a sphere of energy swirling with many pictures, colors, emotions, and ideas inside it. Some of the colors filled me with joy, while other colors nearly brought me to tears. The pictures, however, were diverse and out of context. I saw a picture of a woman holding a child. Her heavy woolen coat and badly worn boots reminded me of an immigrant seeking the streets of milk and honey only to find bitterness and cold. Another image depicted a Native-American boy lazing by a river. He was refreshing himself in the cool waters when I heard his mother calling him. He quickly retreated back to the community where he was reprimanded for leaving his duties. The last image was of Egypt. I could see a large temple dedicated to the traditions of the sun and the traditions of the moon. I could see many priests and high priestesses inside frightened by the Roman army that awaited them outside.

In that moment of consciousness, I understood that I was glimpsing a look at the multidimensional expressions of this one individual soul. I understood this soul's emotions and its reasons for being. I also understood that although these expressions seemed to be mired in a specific period of time, the energy of these times was still alive and influencing the way in which this soul was operating in its present day incarnation. As a person, the colors within this individual soul felt heavy and hurt; this soul was tired of always doing the right thing, and frightened of what the world might think if they really knew who he was deep inside. I could hear this soul crying out to God wondering why he had been forsaken.

This individual didn't seem to be in heaven at all. I drew myself back again viewing the entire planet and the webbing when I noticed something even more interesting. The individual soul I had glimpsed was not the only soul feeling disconnected and alone. Much to my surprise, a large majority of the individual souls felt isolated and abandoned as they all lit up with the same tone and hue. My heart ached for these souls. They had no idea that the magic of the universe rested inside them as they felt trapped by their lives.

When my exploration ended, I no longer felt the room was larger than my body, and I was operating consciously in my third-dimensional reality. Still, the idea that so many souls felt lost would stick with me forever. Most people feel disempowered to make change. Most people feel subject to their life, and not in charge of it. However, what I learned about myself as a dimensional being was that the perspective I hold in my higher fifth-dimensional self alters the intent in the fourth dimension, which manifests as change in the third dimension. Now that I had access to my higher fifth-dimensional self, I could take charge over creating my heaven or my hell, which apparently was my rite.

My observation of the multidimensionality of the soul taught me that as souls we have a personal, as well as collective, orientation. Who we are personally affects the collective consciousness, and the collective consciousness affects who we are personally. I learned that I could change my orientation in the collective from forsaken to accepted at any moment, thereby changing my current reality while lending sway to the collective to do the same. All that was required was to isolate the pictures in my soul's field that represented separation and joylessness, and replace them with a picture of connection and acceptance. If I could change my own pictures, I would be helping the collective be able to do the same thing.

The third-dimensional human quest to date has been a search for the Creator. We want to know where it is we come from and why we are here. From a third-dimensional perspective, we see ourselves as separate from one another, and therefore, we feel separated from our Source and we grieve the loss of our Divinity. Not to mention we are led to believe that the Creator is something outside of ourselves, which only deepens our separation to the point of feeling abandoned. Some turn to religious pursuits to find what is missing, while others reject the idea of a Creator altogether in an attempt to negate what they are missing. Regardless of the position one takes, fear is the only perpetuated ideal in this third-dimension illusion of separation. We feel lost and we do not know who to trust so we do not trust anyone, including ourselves. Mistrust becomes a projection, and manipulation becomes the game.

However, it seems humanity's Creator quest has changed with the shifting times. We are no longer seeking the Creator; rather, we are learning to understand our part in the whole and that we are all unique reflections of the Creator and that it is our responsibility to co-create the reality we desire. Part of our shift into higher being means changing our perspective from one of third-dimensional reality into a fourth- and fifth-dimensional reality that operates both independently, yet collectively, toward the greatest good of all. As souls, we are currently anchored into the physical third dimension; however, our journey during these times is to move upwardly through the fourth- and into the fifth-dimensional planes. In that shift of raising our consciousness climate, the soul will be anchored both in the body and in the higher perspective of our spirit, thereby creating a world of balance, peace, and harmony—otherwise known as heaven on earth.

The Energetic Climate of Matching Pictures

When I viewed the soul and witnessed the pictures in its field, I realized that my soul also carried imprints from previous lifetimes in my field. What I have since come to learn is that we all have the same types of impressions, or what the clairvoyant industry calls *matching pictures,* in our personal chakra field. For instance, when I saw the image of the immigrant woman holding her child, I realized that I, too, had pictures in my field that represented poverty and strife. When I witnessed the Native-American boy slacking in his duties, I knew that I, too, had a picture of being a daydreamer and wanting something more. And I could only guess the number was high as to how many lifetimes I had endured the repercussions of faith versus tyranny. What is important to remember here is that because our souls have lived many lifetimes, we all have run the gamut of experience. We have all been on the winning and losing side of every human dynamic. We have been indigent, and we have been indulgent. We have been diligent, and we have been lazy. We have been feminine, and we have been masculine. We have been Muslim, Hindu, Pagan, Gnostic, and Hebrew, not to mention socialistic, communistic, capitalistic, and ritualistic. We have been it *all,* which is the reason our souls have matching pictures.

What is crucial about these matching pictures is that they suddenly level the playing field. No longer can we judge another for we have done and are the same. By understanding the matching pictures in our space, we provide ourselves access to shift out of judgment and into acceptance. Think of the repercussions that this type of quantum knowledge would have on the masses. If we were to educate everyone on their total need, or how to maintain balance emotionally, mentally, physically, spiritually, individually, and collectively, they would understand how to view their matching pictures and would quickly learn to accept and get along with everyone else. Suddenly world peace doesn't seem so far-fetched. The next two techniques presented will enable you to begin clairvoyantly viewing the state of your soul as you start to become familiar with your multidimensionality.

Technique:
Introduction to Clairvoyant Reading

As you have learned to generate your field, and as you have been using your clairvoyant skills to sense how your field operates, you can now begin actively viewing the many imprints, emotions, and memories that your soul houses within your field. The reading screen is a clairvoyant tool that provides you with a point of focus and allows you to clearly view the energies you wish to observe. Just like Nostradamus gazed into a scrying bowl filled with water and interpreted the images he saw, your reading screen will serve as your focal point so you can interpret the symbolism of what you see. I use my reading screen every day in my clairvoyant practice. It serves to hone my abilities by setting the foundation for inner wisdom, clarity, and focus.

You can view anything on your reading screen. For instance, you can project your vehicle on the screen. Maybe you want to know if your car is functioning properly prior to taking it to the mechanic for a check-up. Energetically you can survey your vehicle on your reading screen looking for any leaks, bad parts, etc., so that you have an understanding of what repairs may or may not be needed. When you get your report back from the mechanic, if what you saw matches what the mechanic sees, then you will probably feel certain that the work needs to be done. However, if you and your mechanic differ as to what is happening with your vehicle, you may want to get a second opinion.

You will use your reading screen in your center-of-head room. In a sense, the reading screen serves as a symbol that lets your spirit know that you wish to view a subject from your own perspective of inner wisdom. The point being, that no other person's or spirit's influence will interfere with your own sense of knowingness. You won't be receiving your messages from spirit guides, or angles, or Nana on the other side; your information will strictly come from yourself. Remember that you have all the knowledge and wisdom inside yourself, and you don't need anyone else to tell you what you know.

Focus Point:
Reading Screen Tool

1. Sit quietly, close your eyes, and go into your center-of-head room. Take a moment to get comfortable.
2. Once you are relaxed, envision a large movie screen dropping down in front of you. This is the screen that will serve as your reading screen.
3. Allow your sixth and seventh chakras, or third eye and crown, to each emit a beam of light activating the screen (something like a using a remote signal to turn on the television). Watch your screen light up.
4. Next, test out your reading screen and see if it is working. Imagine a house up on your screen. Take note of its size, color, and design. Once you've examined the house, take the image off your screen and destroy it, letting it go back into a pure energetic state of potential.
5. Next, create an image of a squirrel up on the screen. Notice what the squirrel's fur and tail look like. What is the squirrel doing? Is it in a tree or on

the ground? When you are done, again release the image, sending it back to pure potential.

6. Now project an image of a plane flying over the ocean. Pay attention to the movement of the plane through the air and the motion of the water in the sea, and then notice the contrast between the two as the plane drifts just above the water. When you are done, destroy the image once again, clearing off your screen.

7. Now that you have tested your screen, and you know that you can "see," go ahead and turn off the screen by disconnecting your sixth and seventh chakras from it (just like turning off the television with a remote).

8. Rest in your center-of-head room for a moment and reflect on all that you experienced before leaving and re-entering your third-dimensional reality.

Technique:
Reading Your Space

Once you know how to activate and operate your reading screen, you can begin to clairvoyantly read the current state of your quantum field. Using the symbol of a rose, you can determine the state of your being or the state of anything that you wish to know.

Focus Point:
Prepare for Reading

1. Begin by grounding, releasing your energy, and filling in your space.

2. Once you are grounded, run your earth and spirit energies; mix them together and bring them up the

body, activating each chakra point as the energy fountains out around you creating your field.

3. Remember to keep your space protected by ensuring that you have your rose boundaries around your field.

4. Once your space is set, close your eyes and enter your center-of-head room. Sit comfortably and pull down your reading screen.

5. Remember to activate it (turn it on) by using your sixth and seventh chakras to send a signal to light up your screen.

Focus Point:
Reading Your Space

1. With your reading screen activated, ask to see a rose up on your screen that represents you in relation to your career (or anything you desire).

2. Take a minute and examine the rose. Notice the richness of its color and feel the texture of the petals.

3. Take a moment to contemplate how this rose looks. Use all your clair abilities to hear, see, sense, and know how this rose seems to you.

4. Examine the bud of the rose. Smell it, feel the petals, sense the vibrations of it, examine the color of the rose, and notice if it is opened or closed. Ask yourself what that tells you about the state of your spirit in relation to your career. Is your spirit thriving or depleting? Is it healthy or in poor condition?

5. Examine the stem. Move your fingers along the stalk, stopping where you might find leaves, thorns,

or knots. Is the stem thick and healthy or dry and brittle? Does it stay on course or curve in other directions? Ask yourself what that tells you about the state of your body in relation to your career. Is your body contented or in fear? Is it living or existing?

6. Determine if your body and spirit are working together or apart. Does the rose connect with its stem? Are they on the same path?

7. After you have thoroughly examined and contemplated the symbolism of your rose, determine if you need to alter your relationship to your career (or other area of focus) so that it is in better alignment with your personal health and well-being.

You may not get all the information you are looking for to begin with, but the point is to become familiar with the process of inward viewing and interpreting the messages from spirit. I suggest practicing reading roses every day. Remember again, when you are first learning to read yourself clairvoyantly, don't feel like you have to make decisions about what you are witnessing, because you are still getting used to seeing inwardly. In the beginning, the importance is allowing yourself to become comfortable using your inner abilities. Over time, you will gain certainty with what you see, and you will be able to act with confidence and make purposeful changes.

6

The Purpose of
Reincarnation

I once did a reading for a couple, a husband and wife, who were very intelligent, witty, and bright people, and were seeking a deeper understanding of themselves. The couple had recently been exploring a new type of belief called the Faith of the Baha'i. I had never heard of this faith before, but they explained to me that it was a spirit-rooted ideal based on the teachings of Abdul Baha'i. They told me that much of what I espoused mirrored the Baha'i teachings, as both were joyful and peace-filled messages meant to empower the individual rather than empowering a structure. The two had a question: according to the couple, the teachings of Baha'i stated that reincarnation does not occur. My teachings, however, spoke often of past lives and reincarnation. Why was there a difference in belief when the messages were so similar? The couple's question intrigued me, and I was curious as to what I would find.

As I clairvoyantly reached out for understanding, what I learned was that the essential message that Baha'i taught was one of Unity in the sense that we are all connected as one soul, whereas the essential message I teach is about the many aspects of the self within the soul. Therefore, in the Baha'i sense, to the soul, reincarnation doesn't exist. The soul is timeless and eternal and therefore reincarnation is not necessary because the soul never ceases to exist, it just is, operating as One in Unity. However, in reference to the self within the soul, or that which consists of our individual inner-workings of spirit, mind, emotions, and body, reincarnation serves as the vehicle for enacting the Creator quest, which in turn leads us to an understanding of our eternal connection to our Source, Oneness, and Unity. For that reason, reincarnation can be both possible while at the same time not being necessary. It is the soul's job to perpetuate life and awareness. The soul accomplishes this goal through reincarnating its spirit, emotions, body, and mind. The eternal part of our soul is referred to as the higher self. The higher self has witnessed, and can recall, all of the lifetimes the soul has lived. When we see what we have been in the past, we have the option of determining whether we still want the same experiences in our future or if we want to change what we have been. This is the healing everyone is seeking today. Yet you cannot heal yourself if you don't know where the cause of the illness originates. Reincarnation is humanity's link back to the truth of its ancient history; it allows us to alter our magnetic patterns and impulses, enabling us to heal our repeating past and create a new future.

If our souls have been incarnating for infinite lifetimes, it's safe to say we are all old souls today. Think about the history of the world and then consider that we have all played a role in what the world is today. Our political, social, economical, and philosophical crises have been created by all of us. We are all responsible for the world's most current problems. But what if the past is exactly what it was supposed to be? Maybe the only thing that needs to change is our perspective of just exactly what our history was all about.

The Design for Evolving into Balance

I have seen a time when earth was new and represented an untapped frontier, ripe with prime creation. Many souls from other star systems saw earth as absolute potential. And they were right. She was unlike what they'd experienced before. She was a free-will planet. She offered abundance, beauty, peace, and more importantly, reconciliation of the feminine and masculine natures. Although earth was a paradise rich with vegetation and water, it was the reconciliation that drew many souls to her even though they knew that it would take ages of time before the ultimate design would be realized. The souls understood that there were principle elements that needed to be seeded into the magnetics of the earth long before balance and reconciliation could be achieved. These were the magnetic principles of light and dark, feminine and masculine, encompassing all that is the duality of the human nature.

The polarities of light and dark had been playing out throughout the universe in varying degrees, and not all necessarily balanced. In order for both the earth and humanity to evolve into their balanced perspective of duality, light and dark first needed to be seeded upon the planet. Eden, the days of the matriarchy, represent the period of light and creativity upon the earth. Today, the days of the patriarchy, represent the period of darkness and destruction upon earth. However, I'm not implying that there is no light today and that there was no dark during the time of light. I simply mean that during the matriarchal and patriarchal cycles, their polarities lent sway to either light or dark even though both were and always are in existence. Earth was the place where no one side (light or dark, masculine or feminine) would reign over the other. The design was for the earth souls to hold a balanced vibration of light and dark. The souls wishing to experience balance agreed to incarnate into the human dynamic on earth as a way to ultimately balance their own dualistic behaviors, even though they knew it would take eons before this balance would ensue. In the meantime, the souls knew they would cycle through a period of light, and then they would cycle through a period of dark prior to the time of reconciliation. The souls understood that the ultimate design for the human dynamic would be to evolve out of oppression and domination and into the higher vibrations of acceptance and cooperation—a shift that can only occur when humanity elected to accept the diversities between the feminine and masculine, light and dark dualistic natures and learned to operate in balance as equals.

The ancients knew that they would transcend their present life only to be reborn into a future life where they would embody a different expression of themselves, time and time again, until which time humanity would rectify its duality. The ancients also knew that reincarnation, with its ability to revisit the past, would be the tool they would use to balance their duality in conjunction with earth's new vibration of reconciliation.

As the souls incarnated into the indigenous population, they set about their journey to remember the purpose of what they had come to achieve. They created calendars and erected monolithic monuments in memory of who they were and their ultimate goal on earth. When the time would come, the souls would remember that the cycle was yet again shifting, marking the time when reconciliation could be had. That time is today and it is through becoming conscious of our many incarnations that we can process through our light and our dark and reconcile into balance today.

The Energetic Climate
of Creation and Destruction

I once did a clairvoyant reading for a woman who wanted to know why she couldn't create anything new in her life. I first reassured her that it was a common issue for most of us. The fact is we generally get in our own way. In this case, my client was getting in her own way by being unwilling to destroy the things that were holding her back from having something new. She was looking for a new career, but wouldn't let go of her fears that she wouldn't be able to find a decent paying job in this tenuous economy. In a sense, her fears were creating her limitations. The remedy? Destroy the fear. In order to create something new in our lives, we have to be willing to destroy the things that are stopping us from progressing.

We've all heard the saying, "Out of chaos comes order." It seems this adage is implying that creation comes from destruction. You have to be willing to rid yourselves of the old in order to have something new. Yet most people I know have a hard time even contemplating destroying something they have created. Yet if you have created for yourselves before, it stands to reason that you can do it again in any way, shape, or form you desire. You simply have to be brave and bold enough to destroy that which no longer serves your greatest good. The problem is that from our third-dimensional perspective we cannot see the infinite potentials that exist beyond, waiting for us to claim our opportunities to have something new. As a result, we usually think we have to "hold on" to all we have created, lest we are never able to create for ourselves again. However, from a fourth- and fifth-dimensional view, there is never a doubt that we can always create something new.

Every time has its time and every time has its end. The time of disharmony is ending, and the time of balance is at hand. With every ending comes a letting go, and with every beginning comes a welcoming in. Creation and destruction are the forces that usher the welcoming in and move the letting go out. Knowing what you want to create and what you want to release during these shifting times becomes crucial as you are establishing new patterns that will enact over the next five thousand years.

Technique:
Chakra Clearing

This exercise is meant to help you understand the energies that reside in your field that are scheduled for destruction today. As you create and destroy energy during this exercise, you are giving your quantum field a well-needed cleaning. Remember to use this exercise whenever you feel overwhelmed so you are releasing the energies that are ready to be let go and opening up to receiving the energies of new creation.

Focus Point:
Get in Your Space

1. Begin this exercise by first performing the basic energy run. Ground, release, fill in, run earth and spirit currents, and pull both your spirit and earth energies up through your body to activate the chakras. Finish by putting your rose boundaries around you.

2. Once you have consciously generated your field and given it protection, move into your center-of-head room and let yourself get comfortable.

Focus Point:
Creation Destruction Chakra Clearing

1. Create a rose out in front of your first chakra, located at the base of the tailbone. Ask that any energy in your first chakra related to poverty, insecurity, fear, and death move out of your field and into the rose. Notice the colors or vibrations of the energies and watch the rose expand as it absorbs them. When the rose is full, simply toss it out into the universe and watch it explode, destroying it so it can go back to pure potential.

2. Next, create a rose out in front of your second chakra, located in the navel. Ask that any energy related to domination, submission, blame, guilt, abandonment, and shame move out of your field and into the rose. Notice the colors or vibrations of

the energies and watch the rose expand as it absorbs them. When the rose is full, simply toss it out into the universe and watch it explode, destroying it so it can go back to pure potential.

3. Create a rose in front of your third chakra, below the rib cage. Ask that any energy related to lack of control, disempowerment, tyranny, strife, and aggression move out of your field and into the rose. Notice the colors or vibrations of the energies and watch the rose expand as it absorbs them. When the rose is full, simply toss it out into the universe and watch it explode, destroying it so it can go back to pure potential.

4. Create a rose in front of your fourth chakra, at your heart. Ask that the energies of self-loathing, hatred, resentment, grief, and anger move out of your field and into the rose. Notice the colors or vibrations of the energies and watch the rose expand as it absorbs them. When the rose is full, simply toss it out into the universe and watch it explode, destroying it so it can go back to pure potential.

5. Create a rose in front of your fifth chakra, at your throat. Ask that the energies of passive-aggressiveness, judgment, criticism, and addiction move out of your field and into the rose. Notice the colors or vibrations of the energies and watch the rose expand as it absorbs them. When the rose is full, simply toss it out into the universe and watch it explode, destroying it so it can go back to pure potential.

6. Create a rose in front of your sixth chakra, your third eye. Ask that the energies of doubt, inadequacy, narrow-mindedness, and rejection move out of your field and into the rose. Notice the colors or vibrations of the energies and watch the rose expand as it absorbs them. When the rose is full, simply toss it out into the universe and watch it explode, destroying it so it can go back to pure potential.

7. Lastly, create a rose in front of your seventh chakra, at your crown. Ask that the energies of mistrust, selfishness, manipulation, separation, and difference move out of your field and into the rose. Notice the colors or vibrations of the energies and watch the rose expand as it absorbs them. When the rose is full, simply toss it out into the universe and watch it explode, destroying it so it can go back to pure potential.

8. To end this chakra clearing, create a large gold sun over the top of your head. Ask that the energies of safety, security, creativity, passion, power, love, truth, faith, and acceptance (anything positive you'd like to bring in) come into your sun. Watch as the sun grows and expands. When it is completely full, pop the sun and fill yourself in from head to toe, radiating with the energies of the new cycle of time.

The energies that you released and filled in with are not the only energies that are housed in your chakras. As you think about all the many incarnations your soul has seen, consider all the energy that is stored in your personal matrix. Clearing energy out of the chakras is an ongoing process. Feel free to run your energy and release anything that no longer serves you and fill in with that which fosters a higher way of being.

7

Karma is the Key to Peace and Reconciliation

Many years ago, I hosted a talk-radio show. I interviewed many guests during that time, but one guest particularly had a large impact on me. I had met Ted at a conference. He was a metaphysic scholar who was extremely intelligent, well spoken, and very kind. Yet, almost immediately, Ted made me feel sick to my stomach. What I didn't know at the time was that in the moment we met, the karma between Ted and I was re-initiating and I would have to excuse myself early from the event. The drive home was excruciating; my stomach was in knots and I could barely focus on the roads. I didn't think it had anything to do with Ted—all I could think of was getting home and crawling up in bed and dying. When I woke up the next morning, I felt fine. I had expected to be aching, chilled, and running a fever, but instead I was energetic and cheerful. It was odd but I wouldn't think about the illness again until one day when I bumped into Ted.

When Ted and I met again, it was a normal day like any other. I was at the store running errands, and again, from out of the blue, my head started spinning and my stomach started churning. I was perplexed as to the cause of my illness, and all I knew was that I needed to go home and lay down. In my harried attempt to leave the store, I turned a corner not looking where I was going and I ran directly into another customer. Much to my surprise, when I looked up Ted was standing in front of me. I was stunned. We greeted one another and talked briefly, all the while I was feeling more and more ill. I finally excused myself and quickly drove home to be sick. Again, the next morning I felt fine.

On the day Ted was to be on the radio show, I once again found myself battling this mysterious illness that came and went with no rhyme or reason … or was there? Something about Ted was causing me to become ill. It seemed to me that Ted and I had some karma that needed to be reconciled. I quietly sat down and entered the Akashic Records to find the karma.

As we, the souls, have evolved through our matriarchal and patriarchal expressions, we have gained a library of experiences. Many people refer to this library as the Akashic Records; it is said to store the accounting of every soul's history, the remembrance of every soul's many incarnations and manifestations. The record hall is a sacred space held in the fourth dimension as energy and information that can be accessed with the use of our clairvoyant senses. Through the Akashic Records we have access to the talents, skills, and tools that we have learned not just in this lifetime, but throughout all our lifetimes. It is widely thought that prodigies like Mozart were accessing a talent they had learned in a previous incarnation. This begs the questions: What if, through mining your Akashic Records, you could find the pictures of your past where you enjoyed love, good health, and prosperity? Could you institute that today?

The Akashic not only serves to retrieve latent or dormant talents, the Akashic can also provide us information regarding our fears and phobias and how they stop us from living our desired lives today. For instance, if you had an overwhelming fear of travel yet you always wanted to see foreign lands, perhaps through mining the Akashic you could target the lifetime where you experienced trauma as a traveler. Your fear of travel may have come from the experience of having a faction bigger than you force you to leave your home in a trail of tears, or perhaps you were a pirate once and made to walk the plank by your captain. Whatever it is that keeps you from living your truest, most authentic self can be healed in that moment as you reach a state of forgiveness by understanding what the event was serving in the long run. This is the healing we all must achieve in order to transcend ourselves and evolve into higher beings. As the earth shifts into her new climate of balance, it will be through the Akashic Records that we souls can find the true story of our past so that we can reconcile it with our present and create a new future; this was my intention with Ted.

As I envisioned the hall of records, a spirit guide appeared who wanted to help me explore the karma between Ted and myself, and I agreed to let her show me the way to our past. She ushered me into a room and I could see a rudimentary laboratory of some kind. There were beakers, test tubes, and elixirs. The era was fifteenth-century Europe. The lab was in a studio flat set above a mercantile. I saw a man mixing the liquids, and I knew the man was Ted. He was an alchemist who mostly made euphoric potions for which the royals paid handsomely. I then saw Ted pick up a vial filled with a bright blue solution as he turned to face the woman who was also in the room. When I looked at the woman I realized she was me. I was Ted's assistant. Ted handed me the vial of blue elixir and I quickly drank it down. Much to my surprise, instead of feeling euphoric, I felt nauseous. Apparently Ted thought I was taking too much of his cut and that I knew too many of his secrete recipes, so he decided to poison me.

I was infuriated at the idea that the reason I was feeling sick when I was around Ted was because he had poisoned me in a previous lifetime. I turned to my guide to see what I was supposed to do about this karma. She said nothing, instead she lead me into another Akashic room. It was a large open space and I immediately recognized it as a court room. *Good,* I thought, *maybe he didn't get away with it after all.* In that moment, all I wanted was revenge and for Ted to suffer the way I had. But I would quickly learn the reality and extent of Ted's and my karma together and it certainly didn't make me feel any better.

An old man stood in the court room with several books strewn about the table in front of him. When I looked at the man's face, I was taken aback upon realizing this man was me. What was going on here? Why was I seeing myself as this staunch and stuffy old man, and what did it have to do with Ted? I was dismayed. I turned to my Akashic guide for clarification. She told me this was sixteenth-century Europe, and that this was my next incarnation after being killed by Ted.

It seemed I was a barrister in charge of determining what books were fit for public consumption. As I watched the barrister, I noticed that one book in particular caught his attention unlike any of the others. It was a simple book with a cloth cover that was tattered and worn. The barrister opened the cover and revealed the name of the author … it was Ted. This was the documentation of the work Ted and I had done together. Yet when the barrister saw the name, an unexplainable emotion came over him. He did not know where the emotion came from, but it was strong and made him uncomfortable, and he even began to feel slightly sick. As a result, the barrister slammed the book shut and banned it from being made public. I was stunned. Could it be that I had once banned books … me, of all people? I am an advocate for sharing knowledge, not suppressing it. How could this be and what did it all mean?

The karma of being betrayed had seeped into the barrister's subconscious, and the repercussion was harsh and immediate. I was suddenly jolted by the thought of how long this dynamic of tit-for-tat had been going on between Ted and me. Regardless of how long this had been happening, I knew I had to change this karmic pattern of betrayal and misuse of power once and for all. I asked my guide and the angels to clear all the karma between Ted and myself as I offered him my forgiveness and understanding. I voiced that I understood how in our previous incarnations we were both living from our egocentric, lower-mind states and that we did not have a touchstone to our spirits at that time. As I was able to find forgiveness for our shortcomings, I suddenly no longer felt anxious about Ted. In spirit, I asked Ted if he could agree to let go of the past and negate our karma; without hesitation, Ted's spirit agreed. Ted's spirit was just as ready to release this debt as I was, and I symbolically broke some sticks and revised our contract in honor of our completed and relinquished karma.

When I ended my journey into the Akashic Records, I felt better. The sickness was gone, and I felt as though I could conduct a good interview with Ted even though he might never consciously know about my clairvoyant recollection of our past. Yet, as fate would have it, the interview was suddenly cancelled when I received a call from Ted telling me he was sick with the stomach flu and wouldn't be able to make it to the show. I told him I wouldn't hold it against him and to call me when he wanted to reschedule. Without a shadow of a doubt, I felt certain that I had reconciled my karma with Ted, and it was now his to process through in whatever way worked best for him. In the end, Ted and I would develop a wonderful working relationship full of respect and appreciation for one another.

Are You Aware of Your Karma?

How many of us are aware of our karma? My bet is that a very small percentage of Americans have any idea what karma is, let alone the ability to recognize it in their relationships. As souls, we have all experienced being the victim and being the aggressor. Karma is the energy that pulled Ted and me together, and it was karma that was tearing up my stomach. Thanks to my intuitive training as a clairvoyant, I was able to negate the past in the present and begin a new future that had nothing to do with petty egocentric ideals.

Karma is often thought of as something that sneaks up on us, rearing its "negative" head when least expected. However, the truth is karma motivates the majority of our actions and reactions. Usually when we feel strongly about something, we can rest assured there is karma involved. The initial intensity of our reactions toward the events in our lives provides us with clues as to the nature of the karma. For instance, when we meet someone for the first time and we have instant rapport with them we say, "I feel like I've known you my entire life." That feeling is karma. Somewhere in your soul's many expressions you have come across this other soul, and so you have recollection of one another even though you may not be aware of the original time and place, or even the events from when you were together before.

How many of us have found Mr. or Ms. Right only to find out a few months later it was all wrong? Karma draws us together, and karma drives us apart. The experiences that caused the karmic connection may not be something we wish to experience again today, yet because we are unaware of the energetic climate affecting our impulses, we are oblivious as to what is actually drawing us together. Perhaps Ms. Right was once your mother who was destitute and was forced to leave you in an orphanage ... what would your feelings toward Ms. Right be then? Or perhaps you were once betrothed to Mr. Right and in that sense he owned you, your will was not your own, and you gave in to a life of submission and oppression. How would that make you feel about Mr. Right today? As souls, the expressions that we have shared in the past may not be the same expressions we want to share today, yet we might still be drawn together to reveal the parts of us that are in need of reconciliation today.

Contrary to what some may believe, not all men want to oppress women nowadays. Men are just as tired of the past as the women are, and the truth is we are all seeking love and companionship. In fact, because the soul has witnessed countless incarnations, we have to remember that it is highly likely that we have been our mother's mother, our father's father, our lover's oppressor, and our lover's healer. Often times, our karmic pasts are resonating with emotions outside of our present day expression; because we don't have a context to explore these sixth-sensory remembrances and feelings, we close off our communications with one another. Suddenly, we feel like Ms. Right is smothering us and demanding that we check in with her several times a day. Or we feel like Mr. Right is causing us to put aside the things that are important to our self in order to, yet again, appease his every need. Resentment starts to build when irrational emotions are held unexpressed, and eventually that resentment builds to the point of rupture. At this point, we will likely find ourselves seeking yet another Mr. or Ms. Right.

Reconciling Our Magnetic Memory

The relationships that we magnetize to our lives are meant to aid us in maintaining that which we wish to grow out of, and that which we wish to grow into. Every person in our lives, positive or negative, is either helping us to grow in a healthy direction or teaching us to detach from our old karmic connections and patterns that no longer serve our highest good. The idea is to recognize the karma and then negate it by first bearing witness to the past, thus changing our relationship to the event. Once we have changed our karmic patterns, our experiences and relationships become more gentle and easy, and we can start to redefine the nature of our relationships just like Ted and I had done.

Karma is the element that was designed to bring the souls into personal and collective balance upon the earth. As we incarnate lifetime after lifetime, a magnetic memory, or karma, would enact. This magnetic force would cause souls to cycle through experiences together over many lifetimes. As a result, the memory of our karmic past would help us achieve reconciliation and balance. Karma would become the magnetizing force by which we would unconsciously become aware of our greater nature and our need to keep it balanced.

It becomes very important today that we understand the role of karma. One of my Buddhist friends describes the law of karma like this:

> *For every event that occurs, there will follow another event whose existence was caused by the first. The second event will be either pleasant or unpleasant based on the intent of the original event. In other words, karma is the cause and effect of our actions, and the intent of which determines the severity of our subsequent experiences.*

Although karma was, is, and always will be the direct result of every action set into motion, we have not needed to fully understand its relevance until today. We didn't need to know the depth of our connectedness as we were mired in our illusion of separation. Today, however, karma becomes our best friend. Karma can help us determine whether our relationships to ourselves and others are freeing or limiting, descending or ascending. Our benefit today is that by viewing our karma, we can negate that which no longer serves our highest good, thereby initiating new circumstances into our lives.

The Energetic Climate of Mirrors

My friend Kendra and I were driving together one day. While we were stopped at a light, a young girl stepped out in front of us walking across the street. The girl was dressed in all black, with black hair, nails, and eyeliner. Kendra looked at me and said, "What's the matter with these kids today, doesn't she know she looks ridiculous."

I turned to Kendra and asked, "What do you think is ridiculous about it?"

Kendra grimaced and replied, "What's so wrong in her privileged American life that she needs to make the statement that everything is dark, bleak, and black?"

I giggled a little but I also understood where her comment was coming from. "You are just mad because she has the self-permission to show the world who she is and you don't," I replied. Kendra knew I was right. Her own inability to have the confidence to live her truth was the resentment she felt for the girl.

As we all have matching pictures, we subsequently all serve as mirrors for one another. The young girl in this story was serving as a mirror, showing Kendra and myself that we needed to reflect upon the idea of living our own lives authentically and not hiding from the world. Part of the re-education we need today is in recognizing that each person in our lives is serving to show us something about ourselves. We may be resistant to their message, but we internally have magnetized them to us so we can see who we are inside. Suddenly it isn't about what someone is doing to us, but about what they are showing us about ourselves.

Technique:
Recognizing Yourself in Others

This exploration allows you to decipher the reflections and messages that other people have for you. This experiment is meant to help you see a face within yourself that you are resistant to see.

As you witness a part of yourself that you consider "flawed," you become more accepting of yourself and the people around you. Consequently, people will respond by becoming more accepting of you, too. The experiment itself is both simple and complex. It is simple because it only requires that you be observant. It is complex because once you observe, you have to make a conscious decision as to what to do with what you saw.

FOCUS POINT:
SEEING OTHERS AS A REFLECTION OF YOURSELF

1. Over a week-long period, observe the people in your life. Ask yourself what you like about them, and what you do not like about them.

2. Next, take what you like about them and notice where you own those qualities too. Then take what you don't like about them, and notice where you are that also. The key is to detect and decipher the message that each person is reflecting to you.

Once you have taken plenty of time to observe what your relationships are showing you about yourself, resolve to amend anything that no longer serves the highest good.

PART III
Finding the Beauty in the Design

8

The Soul's Plan for Growth

I once posed the concept to my mother that we pick our parents. As souls, we devise a plan for ourselves prior to incarnating that includes deciding what family we will be born into. After sharing this with my mother, she scoffed at me rolling her eyes and saying, "That can't be. I would never have picked my parents." She couldn't understand why she would pick her parents as opposed to any others. Why wouldn't she pick a mother and father who would lavish her with love and affection? Why wouldn't she pick circumstances that would afford her a life of comfort and ease? More importantly, why would she ever willingly choose to live through sadness, loneliness, death, and abandonment? The answer is growth.

For my mother, her circumstances of sadness, loneliness, death, and abandonment were part of her soul's design meant to teach her how to be responsible for her own happiness. My mother's soul designed a plan where, in this lifetime, she would be learning that it is not what you receive outwardly that makes you happy; it is what you acknowledge inwardly that fills you up. Her soul had agreed to experience the environment of lack of affection so she would learn to give affection to herself. From there, she would give affection to her children, thereby changing the pattern from whence she came.

In applying self-affection by fostering her desires and her dreams, she would find the one true source of ever-abundant happiness. My mother's soul had designed a plan in which she would learn how to claim the experiences in her life that brought her joy and fulfillment. Her growth would come when she could create for herself the happiness she was seeking, and in that sense, she would have adapted to her environment while allowing her true nature to shine forth.

I have seen on many occasions with my clients how we make our agreements prior to incarnation. As a clairvoyant, I have viewed this planning phase for many people. What I have come to understand is that each soul has a personal plan and a collective plan for growth, depending on where that soul is in its stage of awareness. As I mentioned earlier, humanity is collectively raising its vibration which is part of everyone's soul's growth today, as our collective growth can be further broken down into individual growth.

Our personal soul's plan not only grows itself but contributes to the expansion of the entire collective. At the same time, if a soul cannot complete its growth plan, it limits the entire collective. Each soul has a personal plan that is meant to usher that soul into expanding consciousness, which in turn brings expansion and awareness to the collective. As we grow personally, we set the example for others in the collective to grow as well. It is important to understand our personal growth plan so that we can learn to master the elements of the human dynamic that will evolve us into wholeness and well-being. If we neglect to understand our plan, then we neglect our Divine right to change our reality. Yet changing realities has nothing to do with physically moving to a new location, or starting a new career or relationship, changing realities has everything to do with finding inner peace.

Evolving Past Personal Limits

Theresa had reached her limit. She was tired and fed up with the dating scene and just wanted to know when her perfect mate would show up. Unfortunately, Theresa held a belief that because she was a lesbian that meant it would be harder for her to find love. I chuckled at the thought. I assured Theresa that every straight woman who had sat in my office wanting the very same thing also thought she was somehow at a disadvantage. I explained to Theresa that her soul had designed her sexual orientation to be of benefit to her, not to bring her disappointment. I suggested that we look at her soul's plan and see why she chose the orientation she did.

I clairvoyantly viewed Theresa's soul at the time she was planning her current incarnation. I watched as Theresa's soul considered the best design for her intended growth. The first things her soul had to take into consideration were two very specific and strong patterns that were influencing the re-occurring circumstances of her life.

Theresa's first and biggest choice to make was whether to be in the feminine body or the masculine body. However, Theresa's soul had two specific tendencies in her karma that would have a dramatic effect on her plan no matter which gender she chose. It seemed that Theresa's masculine nature didn't know how to say no to authority and was easily dominated by other people's agendas. As a result, her masculine incarnations resulted in predominantly becoming a soldier and fighting someone else's battles. Her masculine nature never established a pattern of first choosing what was in his own best interest. On the flip side, Theresa's feminine essence couldn't choose what was in her own best interest either. When Theresa incarnated into the feminine dynamic she would become submissive and demure, and the only role she ever played was that of the mother foregoing fulfilling her own destiny.

Both these karmic elements of Theresa's masculine and the feminine natures were powerless to change their circumstances and eventually they grew resentful of their natures for not being able to change their plight. This caused Theresa's spirit and body to develop a belief in self-loathing, which was the karma the soul now needed to accommodate in its plan.

Theresa's soul recognized that the masculine and feminine tendencies toward domination and submission were going to be difficult factors to overcome. So, her soul would design a plan meant to cause her to learn to accept and love herself first and foremost. It was at that moment that the soul decided that the feminine orientation would be best because it was gentler and kinder, but the soul would orient the feminine to its masculine perception because it was tough and poised to hold its position. As a result of this unique orientation, it would cause Theresa to prefer women over men as this would lessen the opportunity for her to give in to motherhood until a time she could claim her desires for herself. If Theresa were a lesbian, at some point she would have to stand up and assert her individual orientation. She wouldn't be able to simply succumb to the social norms. Instead she would have to claim what was and what was not right for her, and in the process she would come to love herself for her strength in living her authenticity.

It never mattered what other people thought of Theresa's orientation because it wasn't for others to accept or not; it was a design meant to teach Theresa how to accept herself, and how to live outside of what our modern society dictates as acceptable or unacceptable. It doesn't matter what anyone else thinks of our personal orientations. It only matters that we live what is the truth of ourselves, sending the message to our collective brothers and sisters that they, too, can live authentically.

The Energetic Climate
of Neutrality and Amusement

The way to overcome prejudice and bias in the world is to teach people the power of neutrality and amusement. As you are learning to view your field clairvoyantly, you will see pictures and ideas about yourself that you like, and some that you don't like. Unfortunately, it's generally the pictures that we are resistant to seeing that represent our greater opportunities for growth. Although it can be difficult to view the starkness of our realities, the way we learn to accept their messages is by clairvoyantly holding our crown in a state of neutrality and amusement.

In this exercise, you will set the frequency of your crown to the colors of neutrality and amusement. When your crown is set to neutrality, you are less likely to judge yourself or others. When your crown is set to amusement, you will be able to find the beauty in any design. I personally use this tool not only when reading for clients, but also when dealing with family and friends just as a measure of good will. The greatest thing about this tool is that you can do it anywhere at any time. You do not have to be in a meditative state to work with this technique. You can be having an argument with your spouse and in that instant turn your crown to neutrality, and before long the two of you will be seeing eye to eye, whether that means solving your issue or agreeing to disagree. You can be at a community radio board member meeting being berated by an angry woman who thinks you have nothing to offer life and society, and you can turn your crown to amusement and find the beauty in her message that is saying, *Be more educational with your content.*

We cannot expect that other people will change to fit our needs. We can, however, alter the perceptions of our need by raising our vibrations and changing how we allow people to affect or control our experiences. You can choose to be in anger and resentment, or you can choose to be in neutrality and amusement. Either way, you are in control of how your experiences affect you, not other people.

Technique:
Setting Your Magnetic Field

The crown represents your seventh chakra, and the last layer of the auric field. This chakra regulates your spirituality, Divinity, beliefs, and authenticity. The crown is associated with your universal identity and orientation to self-wisdom. This is why the seventh chakra also serves the purpose of wearing the face that you share with the world. It is important that you be in charge of your crown so you can operate of your own free will.

The crown constantly cycles through an array of tones and hues. Part of our quantum maintenance requires taking charge of our crown and purposefully setting the tones and hues to the vibrations that match our most-balanced position. What I have found is that using the colors of neutrality and amusement achieves this delicate balance, and this allows us to operate from our highest good. There are many other higher vibrations you can use, such as enthusiasm, graciousness, compassion, elation, generosity, ecstasy, and even simplicity. Basically any vibration that brings you to the positive peak of any experience serves the highest good.

Later in the section's techniques you will have the opportunity to view your pre-birth plan. In order to open you up to these larger ideals, neutrality and amusement are a necessary component, as they can gently aid you in understanding your bigger picture.

FOCUS POINT:
GET IN YOUR SPACE
1. Begin this exercise by first performing the basic
    energy run. Ground, release, fill in, run earth
    and spirit currents, and pull both your spirit and
    earth energy up through your body to activate the

chakras. Finish by putting your rose boundaries around you and setting your space.

2. Once you have consciously generated your field and given it protection, move into your center-of-head room and let yourself get comfortable.

Focus Point:
Seventh-Chakra Crown

1. As you are seated in your room, envision a halo above you that sits in your seventh chakra just above your head. Play with your crown for a moment so you become familiar with its many different dispositions. State that you would like the halo to take on whatever colors you specify.

2. Then turn the halo to a royal blue color. Notice how the royal blue makes your body and spirit feel. Do you feel heavy and grounded, or perhaps light and unrestricted? Remember, whatever you feel is correct.

3. Next turn the halo to a light green color. Notice again how you feel about the color green. Does it make you feel happy and healed, or perhaps, sullen and angry? Sit with the hue a moment before moving to the next color.

4. When you are ready, try a color like hot pink in the halo. Notice how long you can stay at that color and if you enjoy the sensations it invokes.

5. Then try the color mahogany, or deep reddish brown. Feel the sensations in your body and notice that with each color change you feel a slight difference in your space.

6. You can also try the colors of gold, platinum, and silver if you wish to experience sensations that vibrate at very high rates of speed.

7. Once you have given your crown a workout, become still and once again place your attention on your halo. Ask that it become whatever color represents neutrality for you. Give yourself permission to accept any color that comes (you can always assign a new color should you find something better down the road). For now, notice how your unique color of neutrality makes your body and spirit feel about the circumstances of your life. Does this neutral color make you feel judged or accepted? Sit with the sensation of being neutral for a moment and contemplate the events of your life from this position.

8. Once you have spent sufficient time with the color of neutrality, ask that your crown become whatever color for you represents amusement. Again, notice how the energy of amusement makes your body and spirit feel about its circumstances. How do you feel about the experiences and lessons you have learned in life?

Once you have explored the colors of neutrality and amusement, you can end this meditation by setting your crown with both colors and then simply going about your day. You will know it's time to reset your crown if you find yourself becoming impatient, angry, or disappointed. Check in with your crown throughout the day and curiously observe the many hues under which it operates, and notice the effect it has on the events around you.

9

Soul Groups
and Their
Agreements

Anybody who has ever watched a soap opera knows that the reality in which the plot and characters revolve becomes its own environment. For instance, all the characters have high-profile careers yet nobody works, and they all spend hours at the ER but nobody ever worries if their insurance will cover it or not. Some characters come and go, dying and resurrecting themselves over eons of time, while others never leave, cycling together through decades of conflict, turmoil, and passion in which their on-again, off-again relationships never find resolution. However, as outlandish as this environment seems, it effectively serves to demonstrate the inner workings of a soul group and how the environment they enact together either does or doesn't sustain their growth.

We all belong to a soul group that consists of a great number of individuals. Soul groups form when a number of souls wishing to take part in a specific collective experience agree (either prior to incarnating, or when we are in our spirits consciously or otherwise) to a scenario, or set of circumstances, to be enacted and the subsequent roles each member will play.

For instance, a group of souls might get together and decide that they want to experience a lifetime of bonding, acceptance, and love. One member would choose to take on the nurturing mother role while another would take the supportive and active father role. Other members would choose to be children, grandparents, aunts, or uncles, all of whom would spend time together accepting each other and loving one another, thereby fulfilling the group's intention.

Over years, decades, and lifetimes, we cycle through relationships with these various characters, taking on different roles and dynamics with each incarnation. Perhaps your mother today was your brother once before, or maybe you were once your father's mother. The point is that in order to achieve growth collectively and personally, we need to go into agreement with other souls who will assist us (and we will assist them) in soul growth and expansion. Each soul group designs a plan meant to be a win-win scenario for all, although I think it's safe to say that not everyone's plan turns out to be a winner. Many of us have forgotten what we agreed upon when designing our plans with one another, while others are still holding onto agreements that no longer serve anyone's best interest. It now becomes imperative for us to recognize our soul group agreements so we can enact something new together today.

Evolving the Human Dynamic

Waris Dirie is a Somali woman who, rather than being sold at the age of thirteen to man five times her age, fled the Somali desert in an attempt to give herself a better life. Little did she know at the time, her life would change drastically for the better in ways she never could have expected. Years after leaving Africa, Waris would fall into a set of circumstances in which her beauty would attract the attention of a world-famous fashion photographer, and before long she would become one of the most sought-after faces in the fashion industry. Life seemed to be looking up as she found herself with a wealth of resource and attention.

Yet as freeing as Waris's life had become, she would never really be free of the dark secret that followed her from her homeland and plagued her every day of her life. Waris never forgot her home and the oppression that her mother, sisters, and nieces were still enduring every day. But mostly, she could not forget that at age three she was subject to the ritual of female genital mutilation. In her biographical movie entitled *Desert Flower*, Waris graphically depicts this ritual in which another female within the family uses a razor to circumcise the young girls. After the ritual is performed, the girls are then sewn up with a thorn and thread to ensure that they stay virgins until they are "opened" by their husbands on their wedding day. Waris not only had this ritual performed on herself, but had also witnessed the ritual performed on her sister who died after the bleeding wouldn't stop. This is what Waris was fleeing but couldn't seem to escape. Consequently, she decided to use her notoriety to bring attention to the issues of feminine human rights, and would one day assume the role of United Nations special ambassador. Over the past three decades, Waris has received numerous humanitarian awards for her efforts to eradicate her homeland's practice.

It would have been easy for Waris to simply forgot her home and the family she once knew, but she wasn't just growing personally... she was personally agreeing to evolve the entire collective. To date, Waris still faces opposition to her goal to educate her people about the health issues that arise for women when such a ritual is performed. Unfortunately, she has been unable to completely eradicate the practice. However, what Waris didn't know was that she never needed to eradicate the process in order to live up to her soul group agreement. She simply needed to be brave enough to change her own reality, and in doing so, she would be setting the example and leading the way for all the women in her soul group to evolve out of their submissive roles and oppressive environment. Waris's soul now carried the information for the entire soul group, and as a result they would all receive the benefit of the work she had done, if not in this lifetime, certainly in subsequent ones to come as they would be evolving beyond their archaic past.

We all have family karma that needs altering. Part of our evolution today requires that we check in with our current soul group and determine whether to continue operating under the same traditions and expectations, or whether it's time to start something new. I recently did this with my own family soul group. I realized that my family group was in need of updating. We were living by the "every man for himself" ideal. Unfortunately, this was the reason so many of us couldn't sustain ourselves. We didn't have proper support systems. I could see that this tradition and expectation that you do everything by yourself without the help of anyone else was actually having an adverse effect in that many of us were feeling alone, unloved, unwanted, and scared. Consequently, many of us were flailing through impoverishment and addiction just trying to fend for ourselves. I decided that wasn't the tradition I was going to be handing down to my sons, and so I took it upon myself to change the core of us, my boys and me, and establish new traditions of unconditional love, acceptance, cooperation, and support. The practice of "every man for himself" quickly changed into "all for one and one for all." This was my contribution to the expansion and evolution of my soul group. Although I desperately wanted all of my family members to buy into our new way of being, not many of them did. It was difficult for me to think that they couldn't see the value in what I was changing. However, I was reminded that every soul has a personal journey, too, and that they have a right to their own timing and experiences.

As souls we are not all evolving at the same rate of speed. Evolution is individual to what we can personally integrate and grow into at any given moment. So when dealing with other souls, we have to take into consideration and honor their personal timing without forcing ours upon them. The soul's only purpose is to perpetuate the continuity of life and awareness, and to be certain that evolution happens in stages.

Soul Stages

The soul has been evolving on earth over great periods of time. As souls, we evolve through the principles of the human dynamic on earth. We have lifetimes of growing through our light and our dark, our masculine and our feminine, and eventually we reach the level of reconciliation and peace representing the apex, to date, of the human dynamic. Each soul is at a different stage of growth depending on when they entered the earth experiment and the karmic impact their subsequent incarnations have had upon their growth. We can break down the soul stages into four categories: new souls, young souls, mature souls, and old souls. Everyone is at some various stage of growth within these periods.

The new souls are first-chakra souls. To clarify, we are all actually old souls, as our essences have been around for eons. When I speak of new souls, I strictly mean souls new to the earth experience. These first-chakra new souls operate mostly from their natural and primal instinct for survival. Some of the first lessons we learn as new souls is how to simply survive. The new soul stage is primal and unforgiving, as it operates under the ideal of survival of the fittest. New souls often do not have bills to worry over and car payments to make because they are still working on meeting their basic needs for food, water, and shelter. Once a soul masters its basic survival, it transcends into a young and vibrant phase.

The young souls are second-chakra souls. These souls have mastered providing for themselves and in the process have come to know how to live in community with others. Second-chakra souls are powered by their lower emotions and raw desires. Oftentimes it causes them to push their passionate agendas onto others, as emotions are a powerful way to manipulate people into believing in our cause.

Mature souls are third-chakra souls. These souls comprise much of modern society today. They operate from sheer force and aggression, projecting their own perceived power as a way to compensate for once having been emotionally manipulated. Third-chakra mature souls don't trust their emotions or their spirits because they cannot be seen or measured. Maturing souls turn to the tangible realities of life as a way to validate their existence. It is no longer about people and community; it is about the ego and money and what that ultimately provides for them.

Lastly, there are fourth-chakra souls, or old souls. The fourth-chakra soul expression is the shift we are all experiencing today as earth alters her ways of being. Earth is moving out of her lower-chakra expressions and coming into her higher vibrations. Old souls are peaceful and loving. Many new babies and children today are fourth-chakra old souls. They operate from a belief of acceptance and cooperation. They are unconditional in their relationships, meaning they are not trying to manipulate people into giving them what they want. Rather, they will want what is best for everyone. These souls are spread out over the globe and are the ambassadors for earth's new world age. There have always been fourth-chakra souls on earth. They were our masters, saints—canonized and martyred—setting the examples for what we would achieve today. No matter where we are in our growth, today, we have the opportunity to quantum leap into a fourth-chakra old-soul higher way of being by embracing our authenticity and having the courage to live our truth just as Waris Dirie has done.

As I understand it, earth is not taking any new clients. The new soul experiences on earth are grandfathering out. If a soul has not experienced the earth in her first-chakra expression, the opportunity would no longer be available because earth is evolving into a higher state of being; humanity has agreed upon this evolution as well. Today's souls have the opportunity to evolve from new souls to old souls overnight, changing the scope of the world.

If we look at the environment that our soul groups have existed within over the last five thousand years, it's easy to see the damage that has been done to the human psyche. As the masses of us have cycled through plagues, enslavement, revolutions, wars, disempowerment, poverty, manipulation, and devastation, it makes perfect sense why we are all tired, unhealthy, stressed, and at the end of our ropes. For most people, every day is just another opportunity for the bottom to drop out. Is it any wonder our structures and ways of living are no longer sustaining us? It seems our soul group agreements are no longer benefiting the group and the time is now to change our contracts to match the new cycle of being.

The Energetic Climate of Contracts

I have had several women recently tell me that prior to their children being conceived, they dreamed about them. One woman particularly told me of dreaming about a small boy, and then a year later she gave birth to a boy. Your soul is constantly going into and out of agreements. When you form your soul's plan, you make contracts with other souls who agree to help you achieve your goals. The women, who dreamed of their children prior to their births, were in the process of finalizing their agreements and contracts together. Unfortunately, not all of our contracts are serving us very well today, and the time is now to change what is archaic into a new design that prompts a foundation of acceptance and empowerment for all people.

What agreements, or contracts, in your life are no longer serving your best interest? Are you agreeing to be the caretaker of everyone else's needs but not your own? Are you agreeing to keep your head down and not rock any boats? Are you agreeing to forego love for the sake of money? Think about the circumstances of your life and ask yourself what contracts are you agreeing to that make up the events of your life. If there is an area of your life that doesn't seem to be honoring the best interest of all, consider what you might like to consciously enact as a new contract today.

If you are no longer willing to be the sacrificial lamb at work, per-haps you want a new contract that says you will now receive the respect of your peers and superiors as you no longer wish to put yourself on the line for everyone else's benefit. Let the universe know that you are claim-ing your right to be taken seriously. Ask that you be given the courage to stand up for yourself when you feel you are being taken advantage of by others. The idea is to recognize which agreements serve us and which tear us down so that we can change them and enact something new.

Technique:
Sacred Reconciliation

The Cathedral of Souls is a sacred space held in your spiritual mind. It is a place to communicate openly and honestly with other souls while achieving reconciliation and forgiveness in all matters. There is nothing you cannot express at the Cathe-dral of Souls. That said, I should mention that The Cathedral is not a place to sway another over to your side of thinking, as that type of counter-intuitive attempt at manipulation will only come back to harm you through the laws of karma. Rather, the Cathedral is a space to seek resolution of our differences without feeling the need to change another person's opinions and ideas. The Cathedral is a cathartic space that allows you to release your past through expression in the present.

I personally use this forum for communication with all the members of my soul group. I communicate my love, but I also communicate my boundaries. If I feel I am hindering someone's growth because of our agreements, I will communicate to him or her that I no longer wish to hold them back. If I am feeling hin-dered by someone in the group, I will express to that person how it makes me feel and why I no longer wish to hold the hindering agreement. When I am in the Cathedral, I will consciously enact new contracts and agreements in honor of both myself and the other person(s), for the highest good of all concerned. When I end a session in this sacred space, I oftentimes send the other person(s) a rose so that his or her spirit knows that I see the beauty in him or her, just as I see the beauty in myself.

I have seen amazing things happen as a result of working in the Cathedral of Souls. Relationships can be transformed overnight. At the very least, a shift will be enacted on a subtle level that will be revealed over time. The best words of advice I can offer about working in the Cathedral is that it is a very individual process; the Cathedral is different for everyone, so give yourself permission to enjoy your experience in the Cathedral knowing that you have full right to express your deepest thoughts. It is also best not to hold an expectation of the outcome. The person you are speaking with may not want to end the contract. Still, you can express your position, write a new contract, and find forgiveness with this person as a gesture for moving forward.

You can bring anyone you want into the Cathedral, even if the person you wish to speak with is no longer living in the physical sense. We still have agreements with family and friends even if they are no longer alive in a body, and these contracts too can be rectified.

Focus Point:
Get In Your Space
1. Begin this exercise by first performing the basic energy run. Ground, release, fill in, run earth and spirit currents to activate the chakras, and always finish by putting your rose boundaries around you.
2. Once you have consciously generated your field and given it protection, move into your center-of-head room and let yourself get comfortable.

1. To enter the Cathedral, find a door on the right side of your room that will lead you out into the galaxies as you traverse the space and time it takes to arrive at the Cathedral.

2. When you arrive, acclimate yourself to your surroundings. What color is the building? What is the size of the structure? Find the front doors to the building, and enter the Cathedral, still observing your surroundings.

3. Next, find the area within the Cathedral that is shaped like a circle and has a flame burning in honor of the communication you will be having; if you can't find it, create it.

4. When you stand at the circle, you can ask your guides or angels to be with you during this process. These guides can also offer you support and understanding if you need it.

5. When you are ready to express yourself, send out a "hello" rose (like making a phone call) to the person(s) you wish to communicate with, and watch as they join you at the circle. If no one shows up, you can still have a conversation. However, I have found that spirits are always open to honest expression.

6. When all the people who need to be at the circle are present, you can begin expressing why you wanted to have this conscious dialog. This is your opportunity to say everything you feel about your circumstances. Remember that happiness is allowed,

as well as anger. The point is to get everything off of your chest.

7. Once you have expressed yourself, listen to what the other person(s) have to say about what you just communicated. Notice what he or she might offer as an explanation for his or her actions. You do not have to condone their actions; keep in mind that you are all operating in spirit, and spirit understands the bigger picture as to why things happen the way they do. Seek your forgiveness from this higher position of understanding.

8. Some of the questions you can be asking yourself throughout the process are: Why did I agree to this experience with this person(s)? What am I learning by going through this experience? How can I let go of this type of pattern from the past? How can I come to forgiveness and move on?

9. As you ask the questions, listen to the answers from your guides and from the people at the circle. Once you have a clear understanding of your circumstances, request that a new contract be enacted that reflects your healed position and details your conscious intent to re-pattern the future.

10. Once you have your new understanding and agreement, you can leave the Cathedral, re-enter your room, and then come out of your meditation.

Upon completing this exercise, pay attention over the next several days as you are likely to see the results of your new contract in your physical reality. Revisit the Cathedral whenever you feel the need.

10

Becoming Aware of Our Soul's Purpose

We've all heard the idiom, "Don't cry over spilled milk." Generally, I live by this creed. However I heard a story that made me rethink this position. The moral of the story suggested we should pay closer attention to the milk lest we miss the opportunity to prevent an unnecessary disaster.

My intern Lauryn worked as a barista with a man named Simon. One day while Lauryn was ringing in an order on the register, she heard a crash behind her and an under-the-breath expletive coming from Simon. She turned to find that he had spilled an entire pitcher of milk. Yet something about Simon's disposition suggested that he wasn't just upset about the milk, rather he was in awe of what he'd just experienced. Simon looked at Lauryn and said, "That was crazy, I knew exactly what was going to happen." He explained that as he was reaching for the milk pitcher, he was having a déjà-vu moment in which he knew the accident was going to occur. Simon mused to Lauryn that it was like watching a train wreck and being powerless to prevent it. "But that's not even the crazy part." Simon continued. "Earlier in the day, I had a flash that I was going to spill the milk, and I did!" It seems Simon had a premonition prior to the déjà vu.

Once Simon recovered from his initial awe, he cleaned up his mess and never thought of the incident again, brushing it off as an odd coincidence. Unfortunately, Simon missed the point. What he was unaware of was that he had just experienced two conscious moments in which he could have changed the intended design and outcome of his reality. Because Simon didn't recognize he was in his fifth-dimensional power, he was unable to alter the circumstances already in motion. The spilled milk could have been a wake-up call for Simon. It was the conscious event that was asking him to pay attention to his free-will ability to work in harmony with his environment.

I once had a similar experience in which I had a flash of myself getting into a car accident. I saw a large red vehicle running into my passenger side door. The vision shook me, and I immediately said to the universe, "That needs to change." I didn't know why this accident was magnetizing to me, but I knew I didn't want to endure its repercussions, and so I altered the course of events instead. I simply stated that I wished to break my agreements with these circumstances, and that whatever lesson I thought I needed from the accident would have to come to me through gentler means in the future.

The next day, as I was driving, a large red SUV was stopped at a side street trying to pull out across traffic. When I saw that the driver of the red vehicle was inching outward, I knew she didn't see me coming. I slowed up my pace and sent a huge energetic rose toward her asking her spirit to wake up and notice me. All of a sudden she turned, making eye contact with me, and I knew she saw me and that she wasn't going to tempt her fate, or mine. Had I not had the earlier premonition, I would never have thought twice about the red vehicle and I never would have slowed down, but instead, I changed the potential outcome by first stating my new intentions, and then staying alert to the circumstances so I could enact a different reality when the time came.

If our soul's purpose is to enact whatever purpose we desire, then it is our soul's purpose to enact our free will. The implications of enacting our free will are enormous, as this enables us to alter the fundamentals of our lives.

Consciously Enacting Free Will

I recently did a reading for my friend Crystal. Prior to Crystal telling me what she needed insight into, I looked at her energy and immediately sensed her heart palpitating. I could feel the frantic rhythm of her heart beat and I knew something wasn't right. I stopped observing her field and immediately asked her what was going on. Crystal's voice quivered as she told me that her friend and next door neighbor, Hope, had just committed suicide. Crystal was devastated; she and Hope where close, and although Crystal knew of Hope's unhappiness, she never suspected that Hope could take her own life.

I realized this reading was going to be intense. My first love committed suicide leaving me to raise our son alone, and I obviously had mixed feeling about the subject. I quickly asked the angels to hold space for us and aid me in maintaining my neutrality. I asked that my guides help me establish a connection to Hope with the intent of understanding and healing. As Hope entered the room, she purposely kept her distance, standing farther back rather than stepping forward, and I felt she was ashamed. As I observed Hope, I noticed that her waif-like physique was withered and worn. She looked like a haggard woman who was powerless to change her circumstances. Hope said all her life she felt like a disappointment. First she was unable to live up to her mother's expectations, which trickled over into being a disappointment to her father, teachers, and even her friends. Seeking solace for her ineptitude, Hope sought out religion to ease her pain. Unfortunately, due to her state of mind, her religious affiliation would only deepen her wounds, eventually pushing her over the edge.

As our thoughts attract our reality, Hope's internal thoughts of unworthiness, shame, and disapproval led her to a lower form of religion that matched her limited ideals and reinforced her fears that she would never be truly worthy in God's eyes. Hope's church preached a sort of fire-and-brimstone ideal of heaven and hell, and spoke often of the coming apocalyptic "end times." Worst of all though, Hope's religion reinforced a belief that as mere humans we are born into sin, and the one thing God hates most of all is sin. In Hope's mind, this meant God hated her too and that she would never be worthy of his love. Hope was living in what she considered her own private hell.

My heart went out to Hope as I witnessed the devastation of her spiritual impoverishment. She had no contact with her inner source as a soul and companion of God. Yet, Hope didn't want me to feel sorry for her. She said to me, "You do not understand, I finally completed what I came here to do and now I'm truly free." I was a bit offended by her comment and it momentarily knocked me out of my neutrality as I wondered how her suicide could ever be considered a good thing. Didn't she realize that her actions would have a lasting impact on the people she left behind? I highly doubted that they were feeling happy and free. But then Hope corrected me. It wasn't the act of suicide that set her free; it was the act of choosing that relinquished her restraints.

All Hope ever needed to learn in life was how to enact her own free will, as that was her soul's design. Hope said, "In that moment, without knowing it, I used my free will and chose to leave this life behind. What I didn't expect was that in enacting my free will, I was fulfilling my life's purpose." Still it seemed like a tragedy to me that Hope had to find out the hard way how to enact her free choice. If she had chosen to accept the truth of herself rather than believing she was somehow a disappointment, she would never have become despondent enough to take her own life.

Hope's story is a reminder that our only sin is in remaining spiritually ignorant. When we are unconscious of our free will, we are subject to the will of others, and their beliefs become our own. However, if we ever desire to achieve peace on earth, we need to educate people about the ideals of spirit, not as a religion, but as a science and a way of being. If we continue to ignore the fact that spirit is a functioning element of the human system, people will always be subject to control and manipulation by outside forces. However, if we teach people to honor the spirit within first, they would instinctively know what belief was right for them (or not right for them). The only reason we have religious zealots in the world is because we do not teach people the power of their own spirit.

Hope sets an example for us all to wake up and learn to live from the higher perspective of our spirits and stop perpetuating our "hell." Had Hope expressed to herself that she was not a disappointment, she would have been enacting her free will and changing her hell into her heaven. The truth is we can raise our point of view, and in so doing create a heaven on earth. As an American society we have this thing called a forty-hour work week, which is really more like seventy hours a week. We fret over our mortgage and rent payments, we worry that our jobs will go away, we have no time for our family and friends, and to top it all off, we put our children into daycares and schools where someone else raises them, feeds them, and teaches them their "moral" values in life. Is it any wonder it all seems to be crashing down around us?

We are a disempowered society that has reached a critical state of dis-ease (an energetic state in which energies are stagnate and not at ease and therefore in a state of dis-ease). If we do not start enacting our free will and standing up for what we believe in our hearts, we might as well elect to give ourselves over to the faction of the day. No longer can we continue to live detached from our spirits because these are the days of enacting our free will and changing our personal status quo.

The Energetic Climate of Free Will

How often do you exercise your free will? When you are at the grocery store and the clerk inadvertently gives you change for a twenty when you only gave him ten, do you say something or do you let it go? How about when it comes time for a raise but your boss has conveniently forgotten you are due for your review, can you assert your free will here? Or how about, when you are at church and you hear a message that doesn't ring true for you, do you accept the faith of another, or can you assert your free will and find the faith and truth in yourself to follow your own beliefs?

All individuals have varying truths, and to be certain we do not all have to believe the same things. My personal truth says, *You can too have too many CSI programs on television.* But ratings would suggest that most other people disagree with me and believe the market should branch out still. I don't know, maybe we need a *CSI—Mexico City*—that might be interesting. We don't have to reject one idea in order for another to become acceptable. We can assert our will without forcing it upon others. I can elect to change the channel when I don't like the programming.

The new world age is calling us to enact our free will and to recognize where we are giving ourselves away. We are now being called to start living our inward truths outwardly. Change will never happen if we don't start living from our own truths. I personally believe that if individuals lived for themselves first, following the path most in alignment with their personal nature, we would find that we have a natural tendency toward peace and understanding. I believe that if everyone lived out their own personal truths, we would all operate very similarly, and the world would be an accepting and loving place.

Think what you could do if you had permission to live the life of your dreams. If you didn't have to worry over money, health, and happiness, what would you achieve? We only stop ourselves from living our desires because we don't feel we will be accepted and loved, and we are conditioned to think acceptance comes by following the truth of others. Revolution doesn't come at the barrel of a gun. It comes by exerting your will and doing what you know is right in your own heart regardless of what others expect you to be.

Technique:
Explore Your Pre-Birth Plan

In this next meditation, you will be guided to exploring your pre-birth plan. You will energetically go back to the moment prior to your conception where you existed as spirit and were choosing the parents and family that best suited your personal soul growth. This exercise can be challenging if you are resistant to the family you grew up with, but it can also allow you to find forgiveness and closure. Regardless of the type of family you grew up in, coming to understand your soul's plan will provide you with a level of awareness you never had before.

I recommend that after completing this exercise and discovering new information, you take the next several days, weeks, or even months to contemplate through your inner wisdom what you have come to know so you fully understand it for yourself.

FOCUS POINT:
GET IN YOUR SPACE AND BE NEUTRAL

1. Begin this exercise by first performing the basic energy run. Ground, release, fill in, and run earth and spirit currents to activate the chakras. Finish by putting your rose boundaries around you.

2. Once you have consciously generated your field and given it protection, move into your center-of-head room and let yourself get comfortable.

3. To prepare for this reading, be sure to set your crown on neutrality and amusement. It can be difficult to view the circumstances of your birth and family choices. Neutrality and amusement will enable you to find the beauty in any design.

4. Once you set your crown, pull down your reading screen and activate it with your sixth and seventh chakras.

FOCUS POINT:
EXPLORING YOUR PRE-BIRTH PLAN

1. When your screen lights up, ask to see yourself in your higher fifth-dimensional form just prior to conception while you are designing your plan for your present incarnation.

2. As you are making your pre-birth plan, notice who you have around you as guidance and assistance.

3. Next, take a look at a sampling of three families: one being the family you have today and the other two being options that would best assist you in your plan for personal and collective growth.

4. Study the circumstance of the three sets of parents witnessing their states of being just prior to your birth. First notice one of the families you didn't incarnate into. Take some time and simply observe their situation. What were their lives like prior to you considering joining them? Where did they live? How did they spend their days, and what did they want out of life? Why did they want a child?

5. When you have an understanding of the first couple and their lives, move on to the next family that you considered but didn't choose. Again ask yourself,

what were their lives like prior to you considering joining them? Where did they live? How did they spend their days, and what did they want out of life? Why did they want a child?

6. After completing the observation of your options, turn to the family that you incarnated into. What were their lives like prior to you joining them? Where did they live? How did they spend their days, and what did they want out of life? Why did they want a child?

7. Once you have an understanding of the state of each couple, take some time to watch and understand as you make your choice of parents. Notice the type of guidance you are receiving and what they have to say about your choices and how they may or may not offer you what you are seeking for the growth of your soul. As you observe yourself making your choices, ask the questions: What did I like about the other two couples that I didn't choose? What didn't I like about the two couples that I didn't choose? What would my life have been like if I had chosen either of the other couples? What did my soul want to experience and grow from in this incarnation? Why were my parents ultimately the best choice for me? What did they have to offer that the other couples did not? How did my mother contribute to my soul's desire for growth? What did she teach me? How did my father contribute to my soul's desire for growth? What did he teach me? What patterns did I wish to change in this incarnation and how

did my parents help me to find that change? Have I achieved the growth my soul desired?

8. After spending some time viewing your pre-birth plan, send a rose of forgiveness, compassion, or love to your parents in recognition of their help in your design.

9. When you are finished, you can disconnect your reading screen and come out of your inner room.

Take the next several days or weeks, or even months, to process through the information you just received. Notice how being conscious of your design aids you in feeling more certain about who you are and what you came here to fulfill.

PART IV
The Influences that Make Up Your Perspective

11

Knowing Your
Dominant
Archetypes

I was a television junky as a kid, and every character I watched I became. I pretended to be Holly going on a routing expedition with my father and brother. I pretended I was Laura Ingalls adventuring out into the prairies. I was even the Road Runner trying to flee the Wile E. Coyote. But my favorite characters to enact were the heroines and superhumans. As an angel I would fight crime and beat the bad guys. As a genie I could blink my eyes and resolve any dispute. And as Wonder Woman, I would defend all evil in the name of those who couldn't defend themselves.

Yet what I didn't know as a child was that the characters I was enacting were the ones most closely aligned to my own internal nature, or what Carl Jung terms archetypes. We all have dominant *archetypes* that we enact every day in our life. For instance, when I sit down to write, I enact the communicator. When I am at the grocery store, I enact the friendly neighbor. Yet the most important archetype I enact is the one I use when I work clairvoyantly with my clients and students. When I am reading or teaching, I enact my higher self or that which serves as the central unifying archetype that organizes all the other archetypes together under one roof.

Archetypes are the innate universal psychic dispositions that form the basic themes of human life. Jung believed the archetypes to be those elements of the collective unconscious that serve to organize, direct, and inform human thought and behavior. In that sense, the archetypes are the driving influence for what becomes the human life cycle, creating patterns and sequences that make up the events and stages of our lives.

According to Jung, archetypes reside within the human collective mind, meaning we all tap into the same universal personality traits. We all have access through the DNA of our collective consciousness to the archetypes of the Father, the Mother, the Wise One, and the Inner Child, just to name a small few. In reality, there are countless archetypes whose themes overlap one another. However, we don't earn archetypes based on our experiences. Rather, we innately have access to them and can embody their behaviors and beliefs at will. But beware … those who are unconscious to their archetypes inadvertently become the quintessential Puppet. If we don't know what archetype we are enacting, then the archetype will enact us.

As a child, my strongest desires were to defend injustice. It makes sense that I would enact the archetypes of the Warrior and the Hero. Unfortunately, I was unconscious to the reasons why I was enacting these characters. As I grew up unconsciously enacting the traits of the Warrior and Hero, I eventually began to believe that people couldn't save themselves. This belief led me to unconsciously tap into the DNA archetype of the Martyr, who was just dying to show people how to stand up for themselves. But one thing I know for sure, the archetype of the Martyr never turns out well for the martyred. The Martyr is an unrealistic goal because no one can save anyone but themselves. We can enact a specific archetype at any moment, but to do so consciously is to properly assert our free will. Living from a higher perspective means consciously taking charge over our archetypes by knowing what we are enacting and becoming the Puppeteer instead of the Puppet.

As we have come to understand our soul's design for growth, we can now comprehend the idea that it is our archetypes that either keep us on track or pull us off course. What archetype do you wear when you are with family versus being at work? What archetypes do you enact when you are with your friends? Does it change when you are around strangers? What archetype do you enact with your partner when there is no one else around? In other words, what archetypes are you wearing and why do you put them on? We tend to be one thing for one person and another for another. It is important to understand when to institute one character over another. For instance, if you are with your children at the beach wearing your angry put-out parent archetype, by consciously acknowledging this person, you can immediately change the mask to one of the playful and loving parent. At the same time, if you come home to find that your children were playing with fire in the basement, nearly burning down the house, the angry and put-out parent suddenly has its proper place.

Being aware of the face we put on and enacting our faces in their proper settings is what Jung referred to as the individuation and integration of the self. Jung also believed that the processes of individuation and integration had a holistic healing effect on people, as it seemed they would become much more harmonious, mature, and responsible after integrating their archetypes. I personally experienced the holistic harmony that Jung refers to after performing an exercise exploring the theories of individuation. The results of this experiment were unexpected; I absolutely found that when I was done, I felt more at peace and in-control of my destiny.

Shifting Archetypes

Part of my explorations into spirit once included performing an exercise meant to individuate my archetypes so that I could integrate a face that aligned more with my desires. The idea of this experiment was to choose an issue in my life that was troubling me and to find the archetypes that were in charge of that issue. Of course I chose money as my subject. Money and I have always had a love–hate relationship. Money may be necessary, in that we need it to survive, but I have never particularly enjoyed the work I had to do just to earn my meager portion of it. However, at the time I was exploring the individuation process, I was at a point in life where I was following my heart and working toward the career of my dreams. I wondered if maybe one of my archetypes was holding me back from experiencing my full financial potential.

I set the intention to explore the archetypes that were having the biggest influence on my ability to attract more income. I closed my eyes and entered a deep clairvoyant state. Soon I saw a woman enter my inward sight. She was dressed in a grayish-black heavy-woolen coat and wore a woolen scarf wrapped around her head and neck to keep her warm. Something about her struck me as familiar but I couldn't put my finger on it. She had a rough exterior and her years wore on her like the waters wore on the canyons. I got the sense that hard labor was her theme. She looked like a woman who was capable of not only doing her own job, but doing the job of a man as well.

When I asked the woman what she thought about money, her response left me feeling saddened and all I wanted was to get as far away from her as I could. She said to me that money was the only thing in life that you can rely on, and that the only way to ensure having enough money was to be willing to work hard for it. This woman spoke with resentment in her voice, and I got the distinct impression that she was alone and that she preferred it that way. I asked her if she had any support in life and she scoffed at me saying, "Stupid girl, love doesn't pay the bills." I recoiled a bit at her harshness yet again sensing a tone of familiarity in her words.

She was implying that you can never rely on family, or the support of others, and so you have to do whatever needs to be done just to survive on your own. Apparently, this woman was a "glass half empty" kind of gal, something I've never considered myself to be. But as she said these things to me, I realized we didn't have the same beliefs. In that moment my knowingness and wisdom was telling me that you can never sustainably accomplish anything without first having the support and nurturing from your family. If we can't rely on the people who love us the most, suddenly the world becomes a sad and lonely place. Family is the first cornerstone to our foundation and ability to be supported and support others in return. I wondered how this could be one of my archetypes. Suddenly I recognized where I had sensed her essence before. Her voice ran throughout all the women in my family as I had heard her echo in my mother's tone all my life.

My mother used to say we came from healthy Russian stock, and this woman was the Russian archetype that represented my female lineage. Just to clarify—naturally this isn't the nature of all Russian women, strictly the ones in my family. I was put off by the thought that this harsh and unyielding expression of a woman existed within my DNA.

I quickly realized that this archetypal woman wasn't just entrenched in my finances; she was entrenched in my core way of being and was creating a joyless, loveless, and struggle-filled life for me. She didn't believe in following her heart, as it was a dog-eat-dog, man's world in which she had succumbed to its demands for sacrifice. Life held no meaning other than strictly surviving. *Haven't we come further than that by now?* I thought. But then I realized she was that part of me that didn't believe in love. She was that part of me that couldn't accept the help and assistance of others. She was that part of me that was fiercely independent and could do everything for herself. Suddenly, I wondered what my instinctive drive for independence was truly costing me. I didn't want to believe I was anything like this woman, yet there I was: single and self-employed, feeling as if life had let me down and the only person I could rely on was me.

I realized that this female archetype didn't believe in happily ever after, and since I was operating with her expression, I too would never have what I desired. That's when I put my foot down, refusing to accept that this was my only fate. Evidently, this inability for the women in my family to trust in the love and the support of one another was causing them to abandon their dreams in lieu of loneliness and hard work— something my mother mirrored in her own life. I realized that at some point, one of the women within my lineage needed to break this cycle of hard work and isolation, and that woman was going to be me. The problem with this old-world belief was that it was shutting me off to my greatest potential out of fear that life wouldn't live up to my expectations. This archetype was causing me to isolate myself when instead I needed to be meeting new people and engaging in new relationships, which was crucial for gaining new clients and ultimately improving my financial position.

Then, as if a light went off, I was suddenly aware that this woman was not the only archetype at my disposal. I also had access to the archetype of the eternal optimist. I had to believe life was more than just living to work and working to die. I believed that life could be meaningful, adventurous, fulfilling, and rewarding. I decided I would adopt a new archetype whose beliefs and behaviors were more aligned with my true self. I now understood the place from which I no longer wished to operate, and in that moment, I decided to consciously integrate an entirely different archetype in place of this core element within myself.

I had once seen a lifetime for myself in which I was the daughter of a wealthy French count, and I asked to see this part of myself again. As the French woman entered, her demeanor was graceful and gentle. She was nothing like the other woman. When I asked her about money, she said "I don't worry about money. Everything is on the count." Well, that was all it took, she was definitely the archetype for me. I jokingly mused about the idea and how ridiculous it seemed; how realistic was it that I could simply pretend to be wealthy and that would somehow correct my core beliefs about money, support, and foundation?

I have to say, when I concluded my individuation and integration process, I didn't have much faith that it would work because I felt like I was making it up. Oh, me of little faith. Somehow I had forgotten that the universe works in mysterious ways. Just after I finished this exercise, my phone began ringing. Before I knew it, I had booked several new clients in a matter of fifteen minutes. At first, my doubt stepped in and I assumed it was all coincidence, but then my spirit had its say, and I quickly realized that my subtle energetic shift away from believing that work had to be hard and oppressive yielded immediate and near-effortless results by which I was completely stunned. I had altered my magnetics, and was suddenly more aligned with my goals and the people who could help me achieve them. What this exercise ultimately taught me was that I was personally responsible for keeping these archetypes balanced and integrated. I was in charge of magnetizing the life that I desired.

The Energetic Climate of Fragments

Shamanism is considered the oldest form of spiritualism known to humankind. Ten shamans believed that soul loss, or shattering, was the biggest culprit for ill health emotionally, physically, mentally, and spiritually. It was believed that when a soul experienced shattering, due to many things such as loss of a loved one, personal trauma, or pain, a piece of the soul detached itself from the whole and become lost in the energy and time in which it was fragmented. Part of the shaman's job was to retrieve the soul fragment and help restore the individual back to their healed and whole state. However, a person would only become healed if they took on the responsibility of reintegrating their fragmented self back into their whole being. In other words, the shaman may have been able to find the fragmented self, but the individual had to take charge over living it for themselves if they truly wished to be healed and whole.

Today, we must all serve as our own shaman and find the pieces of ourselves that are wounded, frightened, lost, and alone. These fragments may have occurred in this lifetime or they may have occurred in past lifetimes, but the shifting times are calling forth the pieces of us that are lost so we can bring them home again. The way to take charge of defragmenting yourself is by simply paying attention to the many archetypes that conduct your behaviors, and finding the ones that are out of alignment with your desires.

In the same way that I found the voice in charge of my financial perspective, you can find the pieces of yourself that are wounded, hurt, isolated, abandoned, etc. Once you find these pieces, you can resolve to release the trauma by learning the lesson of your strife and then finding a new perspective that better suits you. Once you find a new perspective, you only need to watch over it to ensure that it stays in place and that you don't revert back to your past fragmenting.

Technique:
Reading Your Archetypes

In this exercise, you will be performing the same exercise I performed when finding my archetypes. As you view your fragmented pieces, you have the opportunity to heal them by bringing them to light and altering them in any way necessary so you can feel whole and in control of your destiny today.

Focus Point:
GET IN YOUR SPACE, BE NEUTRAL,
TURN ON YOUR READING SCREEN

1. As always, begin this exercise by first performing the basic energy run. Ground, release, fill in, and run earth and spirit currents to activate the chakras. Finish by putting your rose boundaries around you, ensuring that you stay safe and protected in your space.

2. Once you have consciously generated your field and given it protection, move into your center-of-head room and let yourself get comfortable and set your crown to neutrality and amusement.

3. Once you set your crown, pull down your reading screen and activate it with your sixth and seventh chakras.

Focus Point:
FIND YOUR FRAGMENTED ARCHETYPES

1. Determine an area in your life that needs healing (money, family, relationships with others, relationship with yourself, career, health, and any wound or trauma).

2. Ask to see the archetype that is enacting this fragmented piece of you. Watch your screen and notice who appears.

3. Notice if this archetype is feminine or masculine; become aware of his or her personality and how it is affecting your issue. Is this person empowered, disempowered, honoring, or dishonoring?

4. Take time to watch how his or her influence affects you in your life. Does it cause you to have positive or negative experiences?

5. Speak to your archetype and listen to his or her beliefs and ideals. Do they align with your own truth and desires? Or are your ideals conflicting?

6. Once you have taken sufficient time to explore your archetypal fragments, decide the best course of action regarding what you are witnessing. Do you need another archetype to take over, or do you need to make new adjustments with the one at hand?

7. If you simply want to make adjustments to your existing fragment, do so by explaining to that piece of yourself why it operates the way it does, and then tell it how you would like it to operate from here on out.

8. If you want to change archetypes altogether, simply invite a new person and get to know why that person is the better choice for you with what you wish to accomplish in your life.

9. When you have finished this exercise, simply turn off your reading screen and come out of your inward reflection. Go about your life as usual, but watch for the subtle energy shifts that indicate your integration was successful. Watch for the old archetype to ensure that it doesn't pop up unexpectedly and reverse the work you have done.

After this exercise, give yourself plenty of time to operate with your newly integrated self and consciously observe the subtle changes that happen around you as a result. Perform this exercise anytime you feel like there is a piece of you that is out of alignment or not cooperating.

12

Recognizing
the Nature of
Your Behaviors

Several years ago, I received a call from my sister Morgan telling me of an experience she'd just had with her five-year-old daughter, Jena. Jena had awakened my sister early in the morning saying there was a woman in her room. Morgan sat up in bewilderment wondering what Jena could be talking about. Jena explained that the woman was gone but she told Jena that she would watch over her and keep her safe. Figuring Jena had been dreaming, Morgan didn't give it another thought as they drifted back to sleep for a couple more hours.

Later that morning, while making breakfast, my sister noticed something peculiar about her daughter. As Jena was waiting for her breakfast, she had begun tapping her fingers on the table, louder and louder with each tap. Before long, the drumming had caught Morgan's attention. "Jena, why are you doing that?" Jena didn't know what she was talking about; she was unaware that she was tapping her fingers until her mother brought it to her attention. "What you are doing with your fingers? The drumming—it's annoying." Morgan explained. Then she began to tell Jena of a story about her late great grandmother who used to tap her fingers on the table just to get everyone's attention. In the middle of telling her story, Morgan was suddenly reminded of the "dream" her daughter had earlier that morning.

In a flash, Morgan ran to retrieve the family photo album. Morgan began showing Jena pictures of the family and asking her if anyone in the pictures matched the woman in her dreams. Soon the young girl had identified the woman from her encounter as her late great grandmother.

What triggers our predispositions? Are the behaviors of our dispositions healthy or draining? In my opinion, we all carry the possibility for all realities within our DNA. For instance, we all have the possibility of having cancer. Yet, for some reason we are swayed toward one disposition versus another. So why do we enact certain dispositions and not others? What determines what gets enacted?

For the most part, we are unconscious as to the traits and behaviors we adopt, as was the case with Jena. She was swayed toward the disposition of drumming because she was being influenced by the energy of another person. In that sense, she was enacting an expression that was not her own; Jena was not living her authentic face. Perhaps if Jena was aware that she was taking on another person's characteristics, she could elect not to allow the influence to affect her. Luckily in Jena's situation, the behavior of drumming served as a reminder that she was safe and protected. Until Jena could learn to manage her own field, it was comforting to know her great grandmother was looking after her.

Think about your traits and behaviors; are they your own? How many times have you caught yourself saying something you thought sounded exactly like your mother? How many times have you caught yourself mimicking your partner's mannerisms and expressions? How many times have we seen alcoholism and abuse run as a theme in a family? This happens because our energies overlap with the energies of others and therefore, we influence one another's behaviors. When we are unaware of what influences our magnetic dispositions, the traits rule us. When we are conscious of the nature of our behaviors, we can elect to remove the influences of others so we are able to live our most authentic and true self.

The Energetic Climate of Personal Responsibility

Not only do you have many archetypes, but you are influenced by the behaviors of others as well. Maintaining a higher perspective and balance within your field requires taking personal responsibility for the nature of your behaviors. What prompts you to act the way you do? When a Hallmark commercial is playing, do you cry, or do you hold it in? As the commercial is playing, are you hearing a voice inside you like a mother saying, *It's ok to cry at something sweet and touching.* Or, do you hear a voice inside you like a brother saying, *Seriously dude, it's just a commercial.* Which voice determines what you do? And what about your own voice, can you distinguish it from the rest? The first trick that the Jedi learns is to hold his space and recognize the essence of other people's energetic influences. When the Jedi is in charge of his own field, he is able to discern his own truth from the opinions and agendas of others.

This is where you can use your clairvoyant senses to determine the many voices and energetic influences that reside within your field. Through the act of clear seeing, hearing, sensing, and knowing, you are taking responsibility for maintaining the integrity of your field and how it operates within the collective. By maintaining your own balance and sovereignty, you are sending a signal to the collective that they can do the same.

Technique:
Who Is in Your Field: Chakra Clearing

In this exercise, you will have the opportunity to view the energies of the people that influence the magnetics of your field. As you recognize these people and their behaviors, you will have the opportunity to clear them out should you so desire. By clearing out other people's energies, you create less interference between you and what you want. In a sense, you can accomplish more because you have more to work with and less to get in the way.

Think of this … when you remove energies from your field, you send them back to those who own the energies. As you are reclaiming your clarity and authenticity by releasing the energy, it is going back to its owner and increasing their clarity and authenticity as well—even though they are completely unaware of what you are doing with your field in relationship to them.

Keep in mind that it is not necessary to perform this exercise all at once. You can work the chakra clearing in any order, at any time, and you can pick specific chakras to work independently should you have an issue with one more than another. For instance, if you don't feel creative in your life, focus on clearing out your second chakra. If you feel uncertain about your ability to make decisions, focus on clearing out your sixth chakra. Remember, part of your responsibility today is to adapt the practice to the style that suits you best. If you have just gotten back from the big family holiday, you might want to take a moment and clear your first chakra, grounding. Or if you have just gotten out of an intense meeting with your boss, you might want to clear him out of your third and seventh chakras so that when you speak to others about the meeting, you are speaking for yourself.

Remember to use all your clair abilities to see, hear, sense, and know. If you have a hard time seeing something, simply listen to the frequency or sense the vibration of the color, and you will come to know what is correct for you.

FOCUS POINT:
GET IN YOUR SPACE, BE NEUTRAL,
ACTIVATE YOUR READING SCREEN

1. Begin this exercise by first performing the basic energy run. Ground, release, fill in, and run earth and spirit currents to activate the chakras. Finish by putting your rose boundaries around you.

2. Once you have consciously generated your field and given it protection, move into your center-of-head room and let yourself get comfortable while setting your crown on neutrality and amusement.

3. Once your crown is set, pull down your reading screen, activating it with your sixth and seventh (higher-perspective) chakras.

FOCUS POINT:
CLEAR OUT FIRST-CHAKRA FOREIGN ENERGY

1. Put an outline of yourself up on your screen.

2. Fill in the color of your outline with the essence of your first chakra or that which regulates your physical body and its sense of safety, security, family, home, finance, health, healing, connection, and grounding. Watch as the colors swirl and revolve within this layer of your aura. Take a moment to simply notice how the energy is moving in your first chakra and consider what type of impact this energy is having on your life. Do the colors promote a feeling of safety, security, support, and well-being? Think of the areas in your life where you want to experience more well-being, safety, and connection;

ask to see the colors, hear the voices, feel the emotions, and come to know the energies that are influencing the stability of your foundation. Listen for the voices of the influences in your field and hear what they think about your ability to create health, home, finance, and security for yourself. Are these voices really yours? Who might they be? As you attune to these vibrations, consider if this energy is helping or hindering you, and whether you believe the same or not. If the energy is hindering you and not helping, you can release it from your field, thereby removing its negative impact from your life.

3. To release the colors, pictures, voices, and emotions that represent foreign energies in your field, simply create a rose out in front of you and command that these things leave your space, becoming absorbed by the rose.

4. When your rose is full, simply toss the rose out into the universe, sending the energy back to pure potential.

5. Put a huge, golden sun above your head. Pour the energies of support, connection, well-being, and acceptance into the sun, watching it grow and expand. Create a new statement for your first chakra, something like, *I believe I am worthy of support and acceptance, and I am safe in the knowing that I am not alone.* When you finish making your statement, watch as its energy also filters into the sun. When the sun is full with your new sense of self, pop it and fill in your first chakra.

6. Take some time over the next few hours and even days to sense how your chakra feels when it's free of foreign influence. The more you are familiar with your own space, the easier it is to detect when something foreign arrives, at which time you can remove it before it ever gets in your way.

7. After completing this clearing, clean off your reading screen and either continue to the next chakra or simply be done.

Focus Point:
Clear Out Second-Chakra Foreign Energy

1. Put an outline of yourself up on your screen.

2. Fill in the color of your outline with the essence of your second chakra or that which regulates your feminine wisdom, lower-emotions, creativity, passion, sexuality, and desire. Watch as the colors swirl and revolve within this layer of your aura. Take a moment to simply notice how the energy is moving in your second chakra and consider what type of impact this energy is having on your life. Do the colors make you feel comfortable or uncomfortable with the idea of asserting your wisdom, creativity, passion, and sexuality? Think of the areas in your life where you want to experience more creative passion or intimate relationship and ask to see the colors, hear the voices, and feel the emotions; come to know the energies that are influencing your desires. Listen for the voices of the influences in your field, and hear what they think about your ability to know what is in your own best interest. Are these voices really yours? Who might

they be? As you attune to these vibrations, consider if this energy is helping or hindering you, and whether you believe the same or not. If the energy is hindering you and not helping, you can release it from your field, thereby removing its negative impact from your life.

3. To release the colors, pictures, voices, and emotions that represent foreign energies in your field, simply create a rose out in front of you and command that these things leave your space, becoming absorbed by the rose.

4. When your rose is full, simply toss the rose out into the universe, sending the energy back to pure potential.

5. Put a huge, golden sun above your head. Pour the energies of wisdom, nurturing, pleasure, and creativity into the sun, watching it grow and expand. Create a new statement for your second chakra, something like, *I am in control of my destiny and desire, and I always know what is in my own best interest.* When you finish making your statement, watch as its energy also filters into the sun. When the sun is full with your new sense of self, pop it and fill in your second chakra.

6. Take some time over the next few hours and even days to sense how your chakra feels when it's free of foreign influence. The more you are familiar with your own space, the easier it is to detect when something foreign arrives, at which time you can remove it before it ever gets in your way.

7. After completing this clean out, clean off your
   reading screen and either continue to the next
   chakra or simply be done.

FOCUS POINT:
CLEAR OUT THIRD-CHAKRA FOREIGN ENERGY

1. Put an outline of yourself up on your screen.
2. Fill in the color of your outline with the essence
   of your third chakra or that which regulates your
   mental body, willpower, force, and focus. Watch
   as the colors swirl and revolve within this layer of
   your aura. Take a moment to simply notice how the
   energy is moving in your third chakra and consider
   what type of impact this energy is having on your
   life. Do the colors make you feel comfortable or
   uncomfortable with the idea of asserting your
   power, knowing your mind, and focusing your
   directives? Think of the areas in your life where you
   want to experience more energy and have more
   focus in your life, and ask to see the colors, hear the
   voices, feel the emotions, and come to know the
   energies that are influencing your power. Listen for
   the voices of the influences in your field and hear
   what they think about your ability to know how to
   best assert or reserve your energies. Are these voices
   really yours? Who might they be? As you attune to
   these vibrations, consider if this energy is helping or
   hindering you, and whether you believe the same or
   not. If the energy is hindering you and not helping,
   you can release it from your field, thereby removing
   its negative impact from your life.

3. To release the colors, pictures, voices, and emotions that represent foreign energies in your field, simply create a rose out in front of you and command that these things leave your space, becoming absorbed by the rose.

4. When your rose is full, simply toss the rose out into the universe, sending the energy back to pure potential.

5. Put a huge, golden sun above your head. Pour the energies of focus, intent, will, and power into the sun, watching it grow and expand. Create a new statement for your third chakra, something like, *I own my power and I know best how and when to use it and how and when to allow other people their power, too.* When you finish making your statement, watch as its energy also filters into the sun. When the sun is full with your new sense of self, pop it and fill in your third chakra.

6. Take some time over the next few hours and even days to sense how your chakra feels when it's free of foreign influence. The more you are familiar with your own space, the easier it is to detect when something foreign arrives, at which time you can remove it before it ever gets in your way.

7. After completing this clean out, clean off your reading screen and either continue to the next chakra or simply be done.

Focus Point:
Clear Out Fourth-Chakra Foreign Energy

1. Put an outline of yourself up on your screen.
2. Fill in the color of your outline with the essence
   of your fourth chakra or that which regulates your
   higher emotions, your ability to follow your dreams,
   and your ability to love others as you love yourself.
   Watch as the colors swirl and revolve within this
   layer of your aura. Take a moment to simply notice
   how the energy is moving in your fourth chakra
   and consider what type of impact this energy is
   having on your life. Do the colors make you feel
   comfortable or uncomfortable with the idea of
   following your passion? Do you feel loved and
   accepted in your life? Think of the areas in your
   life where you want to experience more acceptance,
   love, and joy, and ask to see the colors, hear the
   voices, feel the emotions, and come to know the
   energies that are influencing your heart. Listen for
   the voices of the influences in your field and hear
   what they think about your ability to love others,
   love yourself, and create the world of your dreams.
   Are these voices really yours? Who might they be?
   As you attune to these vibrations, consider if this
   energy is helping or hindering you, and whether you
   believe the same or not. If the energy is hindering
   you and not helping, you can release it from your
   field, thereby removing its negative impact from
   your life.

3. To release the colors, pictures, voices, and emotions that represent foreign energies in your field, simply create a rose out in front of you and command that these things leave your space, becoming absorbed by the rose.

4. When your rose is full, simply toss the rose out into the universe, sending the energy back to pure potential.

5. Put a huge, golden sun above your head. Pour the energies of unconditional love, self-respect, focus, intent, will, and power into the sun, watching it grow and expand. Create a new statement for your fourth chakra, something like, *I feel confident that love is the source of all things and that with love I can create my hopes and dreams.* When you finish making your statement, watch as its energy also filters into the sun. When the sun is full with your new sense of self, pop it and fill in your fourth chakra.

6. Take some time over the next few hours and even days to sense how your chakra feels when it's free of foreign influence. The more you are familiar with your own space, the easier it is to detect when something foreign arrives, at which time you can remove it before it ever gets in your way.

7. After completing this clean out, clean off your reading screen and either continue to the next chakra or simply be done.

FOCUS POINT:
CLEAR OUT FIFTH-CHAKRA FOREIGN ENERGY

1. Put an outline of yourself up on your screen.
2. Fill in the color of your outline with the essence of
   your fifth chakra or that which regulates your throat
   and its ability to hear the truth, speak the truth, and
   know the truth of yourself while honoring the truth
   of others. Watch as the colors swirl and revolve
   within this layer of your aura. Take a moment to
   simply notice how the energy is moving in your
   fifth chakra and consider what type of impact this
   energy is having on your life. Do the colors make
   you feel comfortable or uncomfortable with the
   idea of speaking your truth and accepting the truth
   of others? Think of the areas in your life where
   you want to experience more balanced and clearer
   communications, and ask to see the colors, hear
   the voices, feel the emotions, and come to know
   the energies that are influencing your truths. Listen
   for the voices of the influences in your field and
   hear what they think about your ability to speak
   truth, hear truth, and know what truth is for you.
   Are these voices really yours? Who might they be?
   As you attune to these vibrations, consider if this
   energy is helping or hindering you, and whether you
   believe the same or not. If the energy is hindering
   you and not helping, you can release it from your
   field, thereby removing its negative impact from
   your life.

3. To release the colors, pictures, voices, and emotions that represent foreign energies in your field, simply create a rose out in front of you and command that these things leave your space, becoming absorbed by the rose.

4. When your rose is full, simply toss the rose out into the universe, sending the energy back to pure potential.

5. Put a huge, golden sun above your head. Pour the energies of trust, truth, honor, and understanding into the sun, watching it grow and expand. Create a new statement for your fifth chakra, something like, *I am confident in my abilities to communicate the truth of myself at all times, while honoring that others have the right to their truth as well.* When you finish making your statement, watch as its energy also filters into the sun. When the sun is full with your new sense of self, pop it and fill in your fifth chakra.

6. Take some time over the next few hours and even days to sense how your chakra feels when it's free of foreign influence. The more you are familiar with your own space, the easier it is to detect when something foreign arrives, at which time you can remove it before it ever gets in your way.

7. After completing this clean out, clean off your reading screen and either continue to the next chakra or simply be done.

Focus Point:
Clear Out Sixth-Chakra Foreign Energy

1. Put an outline of yourself up on your screen.

2. Fill in the color of your outline with the essence
   of your sixth chakra or that which regulates your
   psychic and intellectual faculties, and represents the
   core of who you are inwardly. Watch as the colors
   swirl and revolve within this layer of your aura.
   Take a moment to simply notice how the energy
   is moving in your sixth chakra and consider what
   type of impact this energy is having on your life. Do
   the colors make you feel confident or unconfident
   with the idea that you can find the answers to
   life's questions inside yourself? Think of the areas
   in your life where you want to experience more
   intuition, knowingness, and validation; ask to see
   the colors, hear the voices, feel the emotions, and
   come to know the energies that are influencing your
   certainty. Listen for the voices of the influences in
   your field and hear what they think about your
   ability to speak to spirit, work within the quantum
   field, and educate yourself about a new way of
   being. Are these voices really yours? Who might they
   be? As you attune to these vibrations, consider if this
   energy is helping or hindering you, and whether you
   believe the same or not. If the energy is hindering
   you and not helping, you can release it from your
   field, thereby removing its negative impact from
   your life.

3. To release the colors, pictures, voices, and emotions that represent foreign energies in your field, simply create a rose out in front of you and command that these things leave your space, becoming absorbed by the rose.

4. When your rose is full, simply toss the rose out into the universe, sending the energy back to pure potential.

5. Put a huge, golden sun above your head. Pour the energies of certainty, clarity, and knowing into the sun, watching it grow and expand. Create a new statement for your sixth chakra, something like, *I have access to the universal magic of life and can conceive and intuit my best course of action.* When you finish making your statement, watch as its energy also filters into the sun. When the sun is full with your new sense of self, pop it and fill in your sixth chakra.

6. Take some time over the next few hours and even days to sense how your chakra feels when it's free of foreign influence. The more you are familiar with your own space, the easier it is to detect when something foreign arrives, at which time you can remove it before it ever gets in your way.

7. After completing this clean out, clean off your reading screen and either continue to the next chakra or simply be done.

FOCUS POINT:
CLEAR OUT SEVENTH-CHAKRA FOREIGN ENERGY

1. Put an outline of yourself up on your screen.
2. Fill in the color of your outline with the essence
   of your seventh chakra or that which regulates the
   face you put on for others to see, your spiritual
   authority, and your connection to the Divine. Watch
   as the colors swirl and revolve within this layer of
   your aura. Take a moment to simply notice how
   the energy is moving in your seventh chakra and
   consider what type of impact this energy is having
   on your life. Do the colors make you feel certain or
   uncertain that you have a right to your one-on-one
   connection to God or Source? Think of the areas
   in your life where you want to experience more
   intuition, knowingness, and validation; ask to see
   the colors, hear the voices, feel the emotions, and
   come to know the energies that are influencing your
   authority. Listen for the voices of the influences
   in your field and hear what they think about your
   ability to be authentic and have a one-on-one
   connection to God or Source. Are these voices really
   yours? Who might they be? As you attune to these
   vibrations, consider if this energy is helping or
   hindering you, and whether you believe the same or
   not. If the energy is hindering you and not helping,
   you can release it from your field, thereby removing
   its negative impact from your life.

3. To release the colors, pictures, voices, and emotions that represent foreign energies in your field, simply create a rose out in front of you and command that these things leave your space becoming absorbed by the rose.

4. When your rose is full, simply toss the rose out into the universe, sending the energy back to pure potential.

5. Put a huge, golden sun above your head. Pour the energies of purpose and authority into the sun, watching it grow and expand. Create a new statement for your seventh chakra, something like, *I am One with my Source, and I have faith in my ability to take command of my own realty and create the world that I envision.* When you finish making your statement, watch as its energy also filters into the sun. When the sun is full with your new sense of self, pop it and fill in your seventh chakra.

6. Take some time over the next few hours and even days to sense how your chakra feels when it's free of foreign influence. The more you are familiar with your own space, the easier it is to detect when something foreign arrives, at which time you can remove it before it ever gets in your way.

7. After completing this clean out, clean off your reading screen and either continue to the next chakra or simply be done.

Perform these clean outs anytime you need. Remember you can do this exercise while sitting in the airport just as easily as you can do it sitting at home quietly by yourself.

13

Identifying
Your Past
Patterns Today

On January 21, 2010, my middle son, Sam, lost the lower half of his right leg when he stepped on an improvised explosive device (IED) in Afghanistan. From the time Sam was born, his one desire in life was to become a marine. His father and I tried to talk him out of it; it wasn't that that we didn't appreciate our service people, we just didn't want to lose our son to the violence of war. But Sam insisted and there would be no talking him out of it. He had his own destiny and the war was going to serve it.

The day we got the call that Sam had been injured was the day all of our lives changed forever. All the disagreements Sam and I had about the purpose of war and what it does or doesn't foster suddenly seemed irrelevant. The only thing that mattered to me was that my son was still alive, and I was bound and determined to keep him that way. In the six weeks that followed, Sam's father and I spent countless hours with him at the Bethesda Memorial Hospital and the Walter Reed National Military Medical Center, ensuring that his many surgeries went well and that his mental, emotional, and spiritual selves were healing, too. So when he said to me that he was planning on going back to Afghanistan once he had his prosthesis, I thought I was going to have a heart attack. Why on earth would he ever want to go back? It made no sense to me. One night, Sam had a dream that told me exactly why he had such a drive to be a warrior.

Sam dreamed that he was a solider in World War II. He was in a large European city and could hear planes flying overhead and bombs falling to the ground. He described hearing the hissing of one of the bombs. He said the explosions were close, and he was frantically trying to find cover when one hit and everything went black. Sam commented that he thought he died in the dream. After his recalling what appeared to be a past life in which he was a soldier who likely died during an invasion, I knew it was time to talk to him about past patterns and the need to change those patterns today.

The patterns of our past have influence over us today. A similar story to Sam's can be found in the book *Soul Survivor* written in 2009, detailing the true story of a seven-year-old boy who has a vivid recollection of his past life as a fighter pilot in World War II. The boy had such a connection to his past lifetime that he recreated the entire cockpit of his fighter jet in his closet so he could re-enact his days of long ago. It is said that we are creatures of habit, and it seems our past patterns would certainly agree. We tend to become conditioned by our experiences, causing us to repeat patterns of being simply because they are familiar, not because they serve our highest good. We all have karmic patterns that we recreate lifetime after lifetime, and until we consciously alter the pattern and create something different, we continue to experience the same.

Part of my job as a clairvoyant is to inform people as to where their seemingly irrational patterns originate, and to help them resolve the patterns so they can create new circumstances. I felt this was Sam's lifetime to change the pattern of being the quintessential warrior, going off to war, and dying for some "noble" cause. During our time at the hospital, I explicitly detailed to Sam that until he willingly choose something other than war, he would continue to experience the same horrific pattern and that this was all he would ever experience of life. Once we understand where our tendencies and patterns come from, we can habituate new patterns that don't repeat the past.

During the many months of Sam's healing and rehabilitation, he took to heart our conversations and completely changed his patterns. He began talking not about war, but about having a family, raising children, and living a long, healthy life. Before long the universe responded. Sam met, fell in love with, and is now married to his physical therapist. Sam now dreams of a future, not a past, something he never did before. Luckily for our entire family, Sam was given a second chance at a life full of love and connection rather than isolation and death.

The Energetic Climate of Programming

The past repeats itself, creating a pattern of being that runs like a program in your space—kind of like the *Sims* video game. Until you consciously change the program, you can never create a new way of being. Do you ever find you attract the same types of relationships, careers, and experiences? Most of us do. This happens because you are meant to notice the pattern so you can change it. This type of change happens internally by taking back your power over your programmed patterning. It doesn't matter what your past patterns have been, it only matters what you do with them in the present. When you are unconscious of your programming, nothing changes; when you become conscious of the program, you can rewrite it into a higher serving pattern that aligns more with your current cycle of growth.

Technique:
Past Life Reading

This exercise will introduce you to a past life so you can begin to determine where your biggest programming comes from and how it influences your current perspective. Be open to seeing, feeling, sensing, and having certainty with what you are recalling. Try not to second guess yourself. You will likely have many similarities today to the past life you are viewing.

The beauty about this process is that you can revisit it at any time. You may at first only get a glimpse of a past life that you don't fully understand. Over time as you revisit the past either in a meditative or contemplative state, you will become more familiar with the details and how this past life has influence over your reality today.

FOCUS POINT:
PREPARE FOR READING

1. Begin by first performing the basic energy run. Ground, release, fill in, run earth and spirit currents to activate the chakras, and finish by putting your rose boundaries around you.
2. Once you have consciously generated your field and given it protection, move into your center-of-head room and let yourself get comfortable.
3. To prepare for this reading, be sure to set your crown on neutrality and amusement. It can be difficult to view the circumstances of your previous birth and family choices; neutrality and amusement will enable you to find the beauty in any design.
4. Once you set your crown, pull down your reading screen and activate it with your sixth and seventh chakras.

Focus Point:
Finding a Past Life

1. Put an outline of yourself up on your screen.

2. Ask to have the colors, images, sensations, words, and vibrations from a past life flow into your outline. Take a minute to observe the energies, watching as the colors swirl and as images float within the space.

3. Find a specific sensation, color, or image that catches your attention. Allow yourself to sit with the energy for a moment and simply feel how it feels to you.

4. Next take that image or vibration and begin to follow it back to its origins in time.

5. Acclimate to this past period of time by first becoming familiar with the landscape.

6. Allow yourself to explore the experiences of this lifetime. The trick here is to be investigative. Is it a cold or warm climate? Are there other people around? What are they doing? Where are you in the scene? Are you a woman or a man? What was your purpose in this lifetime? Did you fulfill it? Are any of the people in your life today with you in that past life? What was their role and agreement with you? How did you feel about yourself in this lifetime? What was the cause of your eventual death? As you investigate your past life, remember that you may not get your answers all at once; it will unfold over a period of time.

7. When you have sufficiently investigated this past lifetime, ask yourself: What patterns from my past

am I recreating today? Determine if these patterns
and programs are serving your best interest or if
they need to be changed. If it is time to rewrite
your program, simply begin to recognize the
past behavior in your life today and resolve to
consciously make a different choice in regard
to the pattern.

8. When you are finished with your past life
investigation, simply come out of your clairvoyant
state and go about your business.

When I uncover a past life, I generally like to take several months
to allow it to develop fully. As I contemplate images of my past, I will
watch my everyday life and see where those patterns are showing up.
As I watch over a period of time, I find that the past life becomes more
vibrant and detailed, lending to the richness of my experience and the
depths at which I can alter my reality.

14

Seeking the
Truth of
Your Beliefs

Many years ago I owned a coffee shop called the Electric Bean. The Bean's original owner had intended the coffeehouse to be a creative hub for "out-of-the-box thinkers." It was this original intent that made the Electric Bean a magical place that carried the essence of transcendence and was the catalyst for changing everyone who indulged in its alchemy whether they wanted to change or not. Everyone who spent time at the Bean at some point felt the push to expand beyond the comfortable boundaries of their lives. I saw my own personal transformation through the Bean, and I know several of my employees had the same type of transcendent experience. The Bean prompted our leap of faith; because of the Bean, we felt that if we didn't "try," we would never know the greater glories of life. The Bean challenged us to question our desires and our paths, steering us toward what was truly in our hearts. Still, I never understood the full power of the Bean until I met James who was a seminary student just out of the nest and was eager to prove himself. James would soon find that the Bean wasn't a place for the faint of heart.

James had been working for me for many months and was proving to be a valuable employee. Unfortunately, one day all that would change. James and I had been working together all day. It was particularly busy and I was glad he was there to assist. James was also very glad to be working that day. He commented to me that even though we were being bombarded with customers, I always had a smile on my face, and usually had their drink ready before they even stepped in the door. He marveled at my ability to know who was coming and what they wanted to drink. He also noted that because I was so friendly and efficient, all of my customers left substantial tips, of which he would be splitting with me. I told him, "Just make your drinks with love and everyone will keep coming back and they will absolutely show you their appreciation." James agreed with the idea and he was looking forward to his lucrative day at the Bean. However, that's when the bottom fell out.

One of my regular customers had come in and while she was paying James for her drink, she commented to me that she was excited about seeing me the next day. I had just started offering private readings as a clairvoyant and she was scheduled for a reading. When she left, James curiously inquired as to what she was coming to see me about and I nonchalantly said, "I am a clairvoyant and I do psychic readings." I could see he was perplexed with the idea, but I didn't give it another thought. I assumed he just didn't know what I was talking about, and I went back to pulling espresso shots. However, James was facing a serious dilemma.

James asked if he could speak with me in private. We went into the kitchen and when I asked him what he needed he lowered his head and said, "I can't work here anymore." I was shocked, I thought the day went well and I asked what had happened. James's eyes filled with tears as he explained. "I can't work for you because of what you do."

What I do? I thought. I asked if he was referring to the fact that I was a clairvoyant. He just nodded his head yes. In that moment I realized that James's beliefs wouldn't allow him to interact with me for fear that I would somehow sway him from his "chosen path." I was dumbfounded and I wondered who had fed him this misinformation. But as I looked at the poor young man standing before me, all I could feel was the torment of his uncertainty. He began to cry and said, "I feel really bad ... you seem so genuine and nice." I had no idea what he expected a clairvoyant to be like, but I could only imagine. To him, I was the devil herself tempting his faith. But in that moment, not even James believed I was the devil. He was torn by what he knew and felt about me versus what he thought he knew about what I was supposed to be. In that moment, James was questioning everything he had been taught.

Although I had been wrongly judged, I mostly felt sad for this young man who was in obvious turmoil regarding his decision. I reassured him that it was brave and honorable of him to come and speak to me about this openly, and that if he felt this was best for him, I understood. I said to him, "I would simply encourage you not to limit yourself but to think beyond just what you've been told about life, and seek the truth for yourself." He just hung his head and cried. I wanted to hug him and let him know it was going to be alright, but I knew I couldn't interfere in this man's growth and learning as he was in that moment recognizing the Divine in everyone.

That was the power of the Bean. It challenged everyone's beliefs and it made us choose again from an expanded perspective. James's belief system had programmed him with a picture of what I was supposed to be, and when I didn't fit that picture, he was dismayed. For the most part, we are all told what to believe and we are not encouraged to seek and find what we believe on our own. Do you think that a young Afghani boy wishes, from the time he emerges from the womb, to be a warrior for the jihad? Belief isn't always our own–it is largely imposed on us. Yet, it is our beliefs that influence our thoughts that create our reality. All of a sudden, our beliefs become extremely important as they have the power to influence the truth of our reality. But belief is a two-way street. Not only are other people's beliefs imposed on us, we also project our beliefs onto others.

Projecting Your Reality

I'm in the business of listening and discerning. I pride myself on being a good listener even though I'm not always perfect at it. Still, I make it my habit to truly pay attention to someone when they are speaking. The reason being is that it is easy to misinterpret someone else's words and then project your own ideas of what is truly being conveyed in the moment. If you have ever played operator as a kid you know how easy it is to misconstrue a message.

For example, I was with a friend one day and we were making cookies. Her husband was trying to get her attention to show her something on the television, but she wasn't listening. Then he made a comment about the woman on the screen saying that her shirt was too small for her frame (to rephrase it politely). Unfortunately for him, my friend had no idea he was talking about the woman on TV, and she thought he was commenting about her and saying she was ridiculously busting out of her *skirt*. She didn't waste any time, whirling around and unleashing a fury on him that made hell look like a good place to visit. I had to interject. She obviously hadn't heard him correctly and was now projecting her insecurities onto him. He didn't say or think anything about her weight. She was the one who perceived herself as something other than desirable even though she wanted to make it out to be his fault. In other words, she was projecting what she thought he thought of her when in fact that was the last thing he would ever think about her.

It is easy to project our sensitivities onto others, especially when we think we are being attacked. But one has to wonder how often we do this when it is not justified and when it is our own illusions that we are perpetuating. Just imagine what a different world it would be if we all became responsible for managing our beliefs and reclaiming our projections. Perhaps we would finally learn how to accept the beliefs of all people without somehow denying the truth of ourselves. The projections of our beliefs have an immediate and direct effect in our lives (similar to what James experienced when I contradicted his perceived projection of me). When we interpret another person's behaviors, we run our thoughts of them through the filter of our beliefs, which immediately influences the ways in which we interact with that person.

The Energetic Climate of Reclaiming Your Beliefs

In truth, belief is mostly programmed into us as a means of keeping us in control. For instance, I had a friend in high school whose mother told her she could get pregnant from kissing boys. Yet, as obviously false as that statement is, my friend didn't know better and believed the myth until one day a handsome boy informed her otherwise.

At some point we have to decide for ourselves, outside of what others tell us, what we do or do not believe. As a matter of fact, questioning our beliefs should be a rite of passage for every individual becoming an adult, because in the end we all must determine for ourselves where to place our faith.

Unfortunately, our society is more prone to persuasion than permission. Most people communicate and convey information through the filter of their personal agendas, and what they derive as belief is simply to justify what they desire. Rarely do people communicate with the best interest of all in mind. This means that only you yourself can really determine what belief is or isn't correct for you, as this is the only way to ensure it is in your own best interest.

Technique:
Defining the Truth of Yourself

In this exercise, you will learn how to reset your chakras so that they are operating from your personal beliefs. This exercise will also use the clairvoyant tool known as a gauge. Gauges allow you to read how much foreign energy makes up your beliefs and can provide you added information.

Remember that you can perform this clean out anytime you feel like you are operating more from other people's beliefs than your own.

FOCUS POINT:
GET IN YOUR SPACE AND BE NEUTRAL

1. Begin this exercise by first performing the basic energy run. Ground, release, fill in, and run earth and spirit currents to activate your chakras. Finish by putting your rose boundaries around you.
2. Once you have consciously generated your field and given it protection, move into your center-of-head room and let yourself get comfortable.
3. To prepare for this reading be sure to set your crown on neutrality and amusement.
4. Once you set your crown, pull down your reading screen and activate it with your sixth and seventh chakras.

FOCUS POINT:
REDEFINING YOUR FIRST-CHAKRA BELIEFS

1. Put an outline of yourself up on your screen.
2. Fill in the color of your outline with the essence of your first-chakra beliefs. Watch as the colors swirl and revolve within this layer of your aura. Take a

moment to simply listen, see, and sense your beliefs and the foreign beliefs of others in your space.

3. Put a gauge up on your screen from zero to one hundred. Ask yourself, *How many of my beliefs in lack, fear, poverty, and injustice are my own energy versus someone else's belief in my space?* Notice the percentage, and then toss your gauge into the universe, letting it go.

4. Put a gauge up on your screen from zero to one hundred. Ask yourself, *How often do I project my beliefs about lack, fear, poverty, and injustice onto others?* Notice the percentage, and then toss the gauge back to the universe.

5. As you attune to the beliefs in your first chakra, consider whether each is helping or hindering you, and whether you still wish to operate under those beliefs.

6. To release the colors, pictures, voices, and emotions in your field that are representative of old beliefs, programming, and projections, simply create a rose out in front of you and command that these things leave your space; they are then absorbed by the rose.

7. When your rose is full, simply toss the rose out into the universe, sending the energy back to pure potential.

8. Finish by asking yourself what you believe about money, home, family, support, safety, security, and foundation. Claim new beliefs by stating something like, *I believe the earth is abundant and can provide for all my needs. I am taken care of. I am supported. I am loved.* Take your new beliefs and pour them into

a sun above your head. Once your sun is full and expanded, fill in your first chakra, taking charge of redefining your beliefs.

Focus Point:
Redefine Your Second-Chakra Beliefs

1. Put an outline of yourself up on your screen.
2. Fill in the color of your outline with the essence of your second-chakra beliefs. Watch as the colors swirl and revolve within this layer of your aura. Take a moment to simply listen, see, and sense your beliefs and the foreign beliefs of others in your space.
3. Put a gauge up on your screen from zero to one hundred. Ask yourself, *How many of my beliefs in creativity, passion, wisdom, submission, shame, and degradation are my own energy versus someone else's belief in my space?* Notice the percentage, then toss your gauge into the universe, letting it go.
4. Put a gauge up on your screen from zero to one hundred. Ask yourself, *How often do I project my beliefs about domination, blame, guilt, lack, fear, poverty, and injustice onto others?* Notice the percentage, then toss the gauge back to the universe.
5. As you attune to the beliefs in your second chakra, consider whether each is helping or hindering you, and whether you still wish to operate under those beliefs.
6. To release the colors, pictures, voices, and emotions in your field that are representative of old beliefs, programming, and projections, simply create a rose out in front of you and command that these things leave your space; they are then absorbed by the rose.

7. When your rose is full, simply toss the rose out into the universe, sending the energy back to pure potential.

8. Finish by asking yourself what you believe about money, home, family, support, safety, security, and foundation. Claim new beliefs by stating something like, *I believe in my right to sovereignty, passion, and wisdom as I create the world of my desires.* Take your new beliefs and pour them into a sun above your head. Once your sun is full and expanded, fill in your second chakra, taking charge of redefining your beliefs.

Focus Point:
Redefine Your Third-Chakra Beliefs

1. Put an outline of yourself up on your screen.

2. Fill in the color of your outline with the essence of your third-chakra beliefs. Watch as the colors swirl and revolve within this layer of your aura. Take a moment to simply listen, see, and sense your beliefs and the foreign beliefs of others in your space.

3. Put a gauge up on your screen from zero to one hundred. Ask yourself, *How many of my beliefs about oppression, domination, control, and use of power are my own energy versus someone else's beliefs in my space?* Notice the percentage, then toss your gauge into the universe, letting it go.

4. Put a gauge up on your screen from zero to one hundred. Ask yourself, *How often do I project my beliefs about power, control, force, and will onto others?* Notice the percentage, then toss the gauge back to the universe.

5. As you attune to the beliefs in your third chakra, consider whether each is helping or hindering you, and whether you still wish to operate under those beliefs.

6. To release the colors, pictures, voices, and emotions in your field that are representative of old beliefs, programming, and projections, simply create a rose out in front of you and command that these things leave your space; they are then absorbed by the rose.

7. When your rose is full, simply toss the rose out into the universe, sending the energy back to pure potential.

8. Finish by asking yourself what you believe about your power, will, force, and focus. Claim new beliefs by stating something like, *I believe I am an all-powerful, spiritual being who can honor the power of others as I honor it in myself.* Take your new beliefs and pour them into a sun above your head. Once your sun is full and expanded, fill in your third chakra, taking charge of redefining your beliefs.

Focus Point:
Redefine Your Fourth-Chakra Beliefs

1. Put an outline of yourself up on your screen.

2. Fill in the color of your outline with the essence of your fourth-chakra beliefs. Watch as the colors swirl and revolve within this layer of your aura. Take a moment to simply listen, see, and sense your beliefs and the foreign beliefs of others in your space.

3. Put a gauge up on your screen from zero to one hundred. Ask yourself, *How many of my beliefs in judgment, difference, hatred, and self-loathing are my*

own energy versus someone else's belief in my space?
Notice the percentage, then toss your gauge into the
universe, letting it go.

4. Put a gauge up on your screen from zero to one
hundred. Ask yourself, *How often do I project my
beliefs about intolerance, hatred, and loathing onto
others?* Notice the percentage, then toss the gauge
back to the universe.

5. As you attune to the beliefs in your fourth chakra,
consider whether each is helping or hindering
you, and whether you still wish to operate under
those beliefs.

6. To release the colors, pictures, voices, and emotions
in your field that are representative of old beliefs,
programming, and projections, simply create a rose
out in front of you and command that these things
leave your space; they are then absorbed by the rose.

7. When your rose is full, simply toss the rose out
into the universe, sending the energy back to
pure potential.

8. Finish by asking yourself what you believe about
your ability to love yourself, love others, and
nurture your desires. Claim new beliefs by stating
something like, *I believe that love is all there is and
we are all the same and what I do to another, I do to
myself, what I do to myself, I do to another.* Take your
new beliefs and pour them into a sun above your
head. Once your sun is full and expanded, fill in
your fourth chakra, taking charge of redefining
your beliefs.

Focus Point:
Redefine Your Fifth-Chakra Beliefs

1. Put an outline of yourself up on your screen.

2. Fill in the color of your outline with the essence of your fifth-chakra beliefs. Watch as the colors swirl and revolve within this layer of your aura. Take a moment to simply listen, see, and sense your beliefs and the foreign beliefs of others in your space.

3. Put a gauge up on your screen from zero to one hundred. Ask yourself, *How many of my beliefs in expectations, communications, mistrust, criticism, resentment, and aggression are my own energy versus someone else's belief in my space?* Notice the percentage, then toss your gauge into the universe, letting it go.

4. Put a gauge up on your screen from zero to one hundred. Ask yourself, *How often do I project my beliefs about mistrust, expectations, and propaganda onto others?* Notice the percentage, then toss the gauge back to the universe.

5. As you attune to the beliefs in your fifth chakra, consider whether each is helping or hindering you, and whether you still wish to operate under those beliefs.

6. To release the colors, pictures, voices, and emotions in your field that are representative of old beliefs, programming, and projections, simply create a rose out in front of you and command that these things leave your space; they are then absorbed by the rose.

7. When your rose is full, simply toss the rose out into the universe, sending the energy back to pure potential.

8. Finish by asking yourself what you believe about your ability to speak the truth of yourself, honor the truth in others, listen to your inner wisdom, and express your emotions. Claim your new beliefs by stating something like, *I believe in my right to speak my truth while I honor the truth in others.* Take your beliefs and pour them into a sun above your head. Once your sun is full and expanded, fill in your fifth chakra with your new beliefs.

FOCUS POINT:
REDEFINE YOUR SIXTH-CHAKRA BELIEFS

1. Put an outline of yourself up on your screen.

2. Fill in the color of your outline with the essence of your sixth-chakra beliefs. Watch as the colors swirl and revolve within this layer of your aura. Take a moment to simply listen, see, and sense your beliefs and the foreign beliefs of others in your space.

3. Put a gauge up on your screen from zero to one hundred. Ask yourself, *How many of my beliefs in terror, doubt, ignorance, and repression are my own energy versus someone else's belief in my space?* Notice the percentage, then toss your gauge into the universe, letting it go.

4. Put a gauge up on your screen from zero to one hundred. Ask yourself, *How often do I project my beliefs about uncertainty, doubt, and ignorance onto others?* Notice the percentage, then toss the gauge back to the universe.

5. As you attune to these beliefs in your sixth chakra, consider whether each is helping or hindering you, and whether you still wish to operate under those beliefs.

6. To release the colors, pictures, voices, and emotions in your field that are representative of old beliefs, programming, and projections, simply create a rose out in front of you and command that these things leave your space; they are then absorbed by the rose.

7. When your rose is full, simply toss the rose out into the universe, sending the energy back to pure potential.

8. Finish by asking yourself what you believe about your ability to access your own information, use your clairvoyant senses, and have certainty over your decisions. Claim your new beliefs by stating something like, *I believe in my right to access the higher wisdom and universal magic available to me through the use of my spirit.* I am in charge of creating my own reality. Take your beliefs and pour them into a sun above your head. Once your sun is full and expanded, fill in your sixth chakra with your new beliefs.

FOCUS POINT:
REDEFINE YOUR SEVENTH-CHAKRA BELIEFS
1. Put an outline of yourself up on your screen.
2. Fill in the color of your outline with the essence of your seventh-chakra beliefs. Watch as the colors swirl and revolve within this layer of your aura. Take a moment to simply listen, see, and sense

your beliefs and the foreign beliefs of others in
your space.

3. Put a gauge up on your screen from zero to one
   hundred. Ask yourself, *How many of my beliefs
   in separation, rejection, disappointment, isolation,
   and spiritual impoverishment are my own energy
   versus someone else's belief in my space?* Notice the
   percentage, then toss your gauge into the universe,
   letting it go.

4. Put a gauge up on your screen from zero to one
   hundred. Ask yourself, *How often do I project my
   beliefs about spirit, God, and Divinity onto others?*
   Notice the percentage then toss the gauge back to
   the universe.

5. As you attune to these beliefs in your seventh
   chakra, consider whether each is helping or
   hindering you, and whether you still wish to operate
   under those beliefs.

6. To release the colors, pictures, voices, and emotions
   in your field that are representative of old beliefs,
   programming, and projections, simply create a rose
   out in front of you and command that these things
   leave your space; they are then absorbed by the rose.

7. When your rose is full, simply toss the rose out
   into the universe, sending the energy back to
   pure potential.

8. Finish by asking yourself what you believe about
   your ability to live your truth, have one-on-one
   connection with the Divine, access your own
   information, use your clairvoyant senses, and have

certainty over your decisions. Claim your new beliefs by stating something like, *I believe that every person has a right to their belief and I honor the belief in every person as I honor it in myself.* Take your new beliefs and pour them into a sun above your head. Once your sun is full and expanded, fill in your seventh chakra with your new beliefs.

PART V
Reinventing
Yourself

15

How to
Heal
Yourself

When I attended clairvoyant school, I had no idea what I was actually getting myself into. I thought I would be going to school and learning how to read people without using my tarot cards. I had been using my psychic skills for a while and was eager to find a new way of reading. However, what I experienced had little to do with reading someone else clairvoyantly, and everything to do with healing myself. At first I was perplexed. I wasn't studying to become a nurse or a doctor. What did healing have to do with clairvoyance? Being naturally curious, I decided to stick around school long enough to find out. It wasn't long before I understood that by clairvoyantly viewing my energetic field, I could determine if my energy was flowing in a state of ease, or if it was not flowing and thereby in a state of dis-ease (the energetic state in which energies are stagnate and not at ease). Should energies remain stagnate for too long, they can become actual disease in the world, whether that be physically, mentally, emotionally, or spiritually. It was suddenly clear that using my clairvoyant skills wasn't about playing parlor tricks and wowing the crowd; rather, it was about me taking personal responsibility toward keeping my energies healed and flowing with ease.

Healing is the first key to our reinvention today. When we look at those parts of us that are in a state of dis-ease and heal them, we reinvent the circumstances of our lives. As we have spoken about the need for a new education of the higher senses, discovered that there is a plan amid the chaos, and discussed the ideas of minimizing the chaos by learning to integrate our many faces and archetypes, it becomes obvious that the soul's only desire during this period of time is for healing. One of the fundamental truths of our quantum reality is that we can restore our quantum field of energy back to its pristine and whole state through the use of our sixth senses, thus enacting instant healing and subsequently reinventing our personal status quo.

Reinvention Through Creative Self-Expression

Skip always had a better-than-average IQ, but no one would know just how far his genius stretched until the day Skip presented the world with one of the greatest inventions of our time. However, long before Skip was recognized for his genius, before he could see his brilliance come to fruition, and before the earth could benefit from his ingenuity, Skip would have to endure a life of pain, nearly succumbing to it in the end. Skip would face the loss of everything he had worked for and he would stare death in the face in an effort to claim a different ideal for himself. Yet had Skip not endured his life's trials, he would never have been in the right place at the right time to spark the inspiration that would transform an entire generation.

Skip had bladder cancer and his odds of survival were not good. He was a very sick man when I first met him, although you never would have guessed it by his appearance and his attitude. He was a man who was younger looking than his fifty-some years let on. His bright blue eyes and genuine smile beamed of light and love. Still, I knew he was trying to make our meeting as easy on me as I was trying to make it on him. He was facing the battle of his life and I only hoped I could bring him some clarity as to why he had designed this illness.

As I sat with Skip, I viewed his soul's plan and realized that his soul had designed the illness to be the catalyst for following his own unique creative passion. Over the ages, Skip's soul had become accustomed to following the directions of others, and so his bladder cancer served as a reminder of the patterns in his life that were keeping him from breaking free of the pack and living a life worthy of his talents.

Skip explained to me that as a young man he gave up his full-ride football scholarship to college to marry his longtime sweetheart and enlist in the army during the Vietnam War. Because of his intellect, he was immediately recognized as an officer and was one of only two members of his seventy-five-person unit to be stationed in Germany instead of Vietnam.

Skip, his wife, and their new daughter lived abroad for several years. Skip enjoyed his life in the military as it afforded him the opportunity to see the world. However, when his tour of duty was complete, Skip's wife missed home and wanted to raise their daughter back in the United States with family. In honor of his wife's wishes, Skip left the military despite his misgivings about letting go of a career he had truly come to enjoy.

When Skip and his family returned home, Skip found work in the construction industry, and even though he didn't wholly enjoy the work, it paid well. Before long, he would become a general contractor working for himself. Skip worked tirelessly, but he prided himself on the fact that he was the sole provider for his family's American Dream. Unfortunately, Skip's laborious life would cause a strain on his marriage, and the two would part when their daughter was a teenager. Skip was devastated, and he knew that no amount of effort was going to bring back what he had lost. Although Skip continued working as a general contractor, the work no longer held any meaning for him as living up to life's expectations only seemed to be letting him down.

Skip would soon meet another woman, and despite his hopefulness that she would bring meaning back to his life, his new wife would prove to be more of a headache than a hope. The only bright spot was the son they would have, but eventually the relationship would end.

Skip felt inadequate, as if he were unable to live up to the expectations of the world around him. He was angry at himself for giving up his scholarship for a military career that he would end up giving away too. He was disappointed in himself for not being able to make the love of his life happy. He was infuriated that he'd married a woman who only used him to get what she wanted. Skip was furious with himself for not having followed the path that was in his own best interest in lieu of living up to the expectations of everyone else.

However, Skip was not in the habit of putting on the "poor me" face, and instead buried his anger. Over time, Skip's self-judgment for never quite meeting the expectations of others or himself would catch up with him. Soon he would be unable to deny what he'd felt for years, as Skip's anger and resentment was collecting as cancer in his bladder. Skip desperately wanted to change his reality. He longed for a career that he enjoyed, a partner he desired, and a life worth living. The only problem was he didn't believe these things were truly possible and the cancer was making him lose all hope. Skip would need to restore his faith in life and living if he was going to beat his cancer once and for all.

As I sat with Skip, I could see that he felt defeated by his circumstances, and I could also see that Skip needed a new direction in life. Skip's body would no longer allow him to work at the back-breaking pace of his past. His physical body needed a new way of working, which meant he would also have to heal his spirit in order to find a new creative expression and purpose in the world.

I asked Skip what he felt impassioned about in life. He slyly smiled and said, "Well, I'm somewhat of an inventor." When I asked what he invented he said, "Just little gizmos and gadgets but there is one thing I'm really passionate about." I immediately viewed Skip's idea to see if it held any validity and what I saw was astounding.

During Skip's long commutes to work he would notice that the wind farm nearby was unable to use its turbines exactly when they were needed most—on high-wind days. It seemed the system was unable to accommodate the force of the winds as it would cause the turbines to move too quickly, which was a hazard for birds, not to mention the fact that the wind farm had no way of storing the excess energy. In a sense, the wind farm was mostly blowing smoke—it couldn't keep up with the very force it was supposed to harness. Luckily for the world, Skip conceived an idea to resolve these issues. To me, his invention looked like a real winner, as it seemed to be exactly what the world needed. But more importantly, it was what Skip needed in order to find a new purpose for living. I encouraged him to follow his ingenuity to make his invention a reality as this could represent the healing that his spirit was seeking. Unfortunately, Skip's world was nearly at an end. He didn't have time to develop his ingenious idea because time was quickly running out.

Several months after first meeting Skip, I learned that his cancer had worsened. Consequently, he would undergo a radical bladder surgery in which doctors would completely rebuild the organ from Skip's own intestines. The doctors didn't give Skip much hope that he would survive the procedure. However, Skip was determined to prove them wrong and he not only endured, but thrived. Though Skip's body was finally on the mend, his spirit still needed addressing if his healing was going to be complete.

When I saw Skip several months after his surgery, he had no idea what his next step in life would be. No one would have ever known it, but in Skip's quest for healing he had lost his entire life's fortune and was nearly destitute. Skip's medical bills had taken all of his life's earnings and the truth was he could no longer work like he did before; even if he could, he no longer wished to strive for the same American Dream that had nearly killed him in the first place. Skip didn't know what would happen next. He was simply happy to be alive. But unless Skip followed through with his spirit's healing, his happiness was sure to be short lived, as his cancer would likely manifest again in a different place. It was then that I was reminded of Skip's innovative idea. His spirit needed a new creative self-expression, and his invention was the cure.

I inquired to Skip as to what he had done with his brilliant idea, as I believed this was the healing his spirit was seeking. However, his reply came as a shock to me. He said, "I don't think that could amount to anything and I haven't really given it a second thought." I was suddenly aware of how conditioned I am into seeing the potential in everyone, even when they can't see it in themselves. However, after our conversation, Skip and his business-savvy son-in-law began to research patents, and soon Skip's invention was becoming a reality. Skip's genius had figured out a way to slow down the blades of the wind turbines and to capture and store the energy so that the farm could operate at full capacity on high-wind days. When Skip presented his patents to the industry engineers, it was said that he had single-handedly revolutionize the energy industry.

Suddenly, Skip's passion for life was transformed, as was his health, wealth, and reason for living. He had followed his spirit's creative self-expression, and as a result he would never need to worry about money and striving to meet the expectation again. Skip had just afforded himself, as well as his entire family and support system, a life of purpose, fulfillment, and joy. Last I saw Skip, he had completely reinvented the circumstances of his life.

Look around today and notice the state of the earth and her environment. There is no doubt that she is in need of healing. If we continue to pollute our life waters and fresh air, if we continue to cut down the healing forests, earth's environment will surely cease to be supportive. Yet the sixth-sense sciences tell us that our outward environment is a direct reflection of our inner environment. So if our physical environment is toxic and dying, what does that say about the state of our inward energies and how we feel about ourselves and others?

In order to change the world, one must first heal the self. The state of the self and its relationship to reality ultimately determines whether energy is at ease or dis-ease. The shifting times are prompting us all to take responsibility for our inner environments, lest we destroy our outer reality.

The Fundamental Truth of Healing

Today, restoring the environment, bringing peace to the earth, and re-inventing our circumstances means first taking charge of our personal healing so that we can reflect healing in the world. As we become conscious of our relationships to the events in our lives, we learn the fundamental truth of healing. Our outward experiences serve as mirrors for our inward relationship to the self, and it is our inward relationship to our self that fundamentally attracts and engages us into states of ease or dis-ease. Therefore, if we heal on the inside, then we experience well-being on the outside.

Healing is a misunderstood art by most Americans. We consider health care to be HMOs, insurance premiums, and pharmaceutical medicines, yet any doctor would tell you that the body is a self-healing mechanism. However, modern medicine teaches us that healing happens via forces outside of the body. We go to a doctor who assesses our physicality and then she gives us some medicine to make it better. The only problem is that we are more than just our physicality. If we break a bone, going to the doctor is the best scenario because doctors treat physical issues. However, prior to there being a physical issue, there may be emotional, mental, or spiritual issues. Sometimes our energy is dis-eased because emotionally we need to speak a truth about ourselves but are resistant to communicating. Sometimes energy is dis-eased because we need to shut down our mental body by being still and listening to our intuition. Other times energy can be dis-eased because our spirits are in need of stepping up and claiming their rightful power, despite the fact we don't always feel worthy of it. And sometimes our bodies hold on to painful memories that must be endured again today in order to be recognized and released.

The point is that illness is energy in a state of dis-ease that happens on many levels. The other point is that we are not educated to seek inner healing; we are taught to defer to something outside of ourselves, except that healing begins by first going inward, meditatively, and speaking to the energy that is in a state of dis-ease. When I spoke to Skip's dis-ease, I realized that although the energy was manifesting in his body, it was actually stagnating in his spirit. In that sense, if he healed his spirit's need, he would be healing himself forever.

What if we could talk to our emotions and give voice to their fears prior to them festering into a cancer or other disease later down the road? When we have the ability to clairvoyantly work with our emotions, minds, bodies, and spirits, then our energy need never stay in a state of dis-ease long enough to manifest itself in the physical body. For instance, when I get a cold and I speak to my illness, I usually find that there is something in my fifth chakra that I need to communicate emotionally of which I am fearful of expressing. As the fifth chakra regulates the ears, nose, throat, and emotional communications, it makes sense that once I give voice to my emotions, my symptoms immediately lessen and I am on the road to recovery.

But to be clear, illness is not a bad thing, and the goal is not to eradicate sickness. Death and dying serve a purpose and are healing in their own rights, too. The goal is to learn to listen to our illness's messages so we can either maintain health and well-being or understand what our illnesses are teaching us. Think about the implications that the ideal of self-healing has on something like the monstrosity we call modern health care. When we educate ourselves about our sixth senses, we learn that we are a self-healing mechanism at which time our ideas of health care become obsolete. All of a sudden we no longer need our insurance industries to regulate our health, because health, healing, and well-being become a simple matter of quantum maintenance, living authentically, and knowing our total need.

The Energetic Climate of Knowing Your Total Need

Think about the areas in your life that need healing. Is your career, relationship, or family killing you? How about the pace at which you live your life? More importantly, are you aware of the many parts of yourself that require healing? In order to reinvent yourself, you must come to know your total need.

The soul exists on many levels, and sickness can reside in any and all of our many selves. If you recall, we each have a higher self (spirit) and a lower self (body), as well as a feminine self and a masculine self. There is also an emotional self, a physical self, a mental self, and a spiritual self within the soul. There is a past, present, and future self that exists not only in the third dimension, but also into the fourth, fifth, sixth, and higher dimensions. And of course there are your many archetypal selves. At this moment, your soul exists in every one of the aforementioned expressions simultaneously, whether you are aware of it or not.

As a spiritual being, you have the energetic charge for both the masculine and the feminine essences regardless of the physical body gender you chose. The fact is you need both masculine and feminine expressions in order to achieve personal balance. What I have come to understand about both of these energetic charges is that the energy of the Divine masculine invokes imagination and exploration, while the energy of the Divine feminine invokes compassion and nurturing. When your masculine and feminine faces are balanced and working in tandem, you are able to conceive and nurture new ideas and new ways of being.

The soul also incorporates four bodies: the mental body, the physical body, the emotional body, and the spiritual body. The mental body is the builder and is the part of you that formulates and reasons. Energy gets stuck in the mental body when you over think your plan and stop allowing inspiration into the equation. The physical body is the form or manifestation and is that part of you that holds density and creates separation. Illness in the physical body happens when you hold memory of pain from the past, or when you severely neglect your mental, emotional, and spiritual bodies. The emotional body is the rudder and is that part of you that is instinctual and intuitive as it strives to keep you on your path. Energy gets stuck in the emotions when you either overexpress or don't communicate your feelings. The spiritual body is the visionary. It is that part of you that is inspiring and allows you to connect with others. It is also all that you have been in the past and all that you are becoming in the future. Spirit also connects you to your creative Source or God. Energy in the spirit can stagnate when you are only following your lower purpose and ignoring your higher perspective.

In our society, we place emphasis on the mental and physical bodies, giving little or no consideration to the emotional body. But most bizarrely is that we completely disassociate from our spiritual body, placing it outside of ourselves and relegating it to the realms of religion when the two are fundamentally different concepts. The bottom line is that the bodies work in tandem and you have to be considerate of each of these bodies if you are going to maintain a balanced position.

There is also the issue of the lower and higher selves that must be balanced. The largest part of our healing today is to bridge the gap between our higher and lower selves. The best way to build this bridge is by understanding what drove the two selves apart in the first place. There is a history between the higher and lower self that must be reconciled if health and well-being are to be sustained. To understand this history, you first have to know how the higher and lower minds function as part of your brain. The brain operates under two hemispheres (right and left). The left brain is the intellectual egotistical mind, and the right brain is the intuitive spirit mind. The intellectual mind is a function of the lower self, which is associated with the physical and mental bodies as well as chakras one, two, and three, and is simply lower in frequency. On the flip side, the intuitive mind is a function of the higher self, which is associated with the emotional and spiritual bodies, as well as chakras four, five, six, and seven, and vibrates at a higher frequency.

Long ago, the two hemispheres separated in consciousness. The higher mind held the all-knowing wisdom consciousness while the lower mind held the fearful and uncertain unconsciousness. The intellectual lower mind, being unconscious as to the source of the intuitive higher mind's information, began to fear the higher mind. This lower-self thinking caused a rift between the two minds. The lower self was afraid of what the higher self might conceive, and it began a cycle of denying and ignoring communication with its partner. Soon, the flow was cut off between the intuitive mind and the intellectual mind. The intellectual mind took command of its five-sense capacities and disregarded the intuitive mind and its sixth sense. The five senses became the dominating force in our reality, as we began to identify and experience each of our selves as separate and alone. The five senses began to structure experiences around fear and separation because they had been cut off from their source, rendering the lower self unable to change its circumstances. The lower self, not realizing the intuitive mind was the source of its inspiration soon become destined to only repeating its past experiences as it could not conceptualize anything new on its own. However, the intuitive higher mind operates in the energetic and informational realities of the fourth and fifth dimensions and serves as the creative force that accesses the infinite supply of possibilities. You need only to recognize your higher mind in order to reinstate your connection to it and bridge the gap back into inspiration.

But don't forget you also live as a past, present, and future self, all of which must be balanced, too. The key to this healing is to simply recognize where your thoughts drift. Are you stuck in the past, or maybe the future? How often do you exist in the present? Strictly living in the present is not always the goal. Sometimes we must revisit the past or set intentions for the future as well. The point is to recognize where you are existing at any moment so you know what you need to do in order to remain balanced in your past, present, and future. Keeping these three items balanced means healing the past by enacting a new pattern in the present that is in alignment with the future you desire. When you find yourself in the past, ask yourself what needs healing. When you find yourself in the future, determine if you are envisioning a positive or negative event and then come back to the present and resolve to eliminate the negativity and start living your higher vision. When you find yourself in the present, appreciate all that you are and all that you are accomplishing.

As for keeping your archetypal selves healed, you simply need keep an eye on who is playing the puppeteer and whether that expression is in your best interest. If it is not, change your mask.

Technique:
Meeting a Healing Guide

You are so much more than just your physical reality. Energy can stagnate in the many parts of you, and the idea is to recognize where your energy is experiencing a state of dis-ease. In this exercise, you will meet a guide who will help you keep track of the many parts of yourself so that you can stay on top of your own healing.

Healing is the essential message of all the techniques. In the case of spirit and your quantum fields, energy that is moving is healed, while energy that is not moving is considered to be in a state of dis-ease. When you perform the healing in this exercise, you may not know why the energy is stagnant, but don't panic or fret. For now, you do not need to know what the energy represents, because it is enough that you just know you can move it and get it back in the flow. As you become more certain in your clairvoyant abilities, you will better understand the reasons energies get stuck. For now, simply acclimate to the idea of being able to view, move, and heal yourself, as well as being able to work with other spirits to achieve your goals.

I always joke that the spirit-guide structure operates a lot like the Verizon Wireless commercials where there is no end to the types of support you have available to you. Some guides serve as runners, finding the things you may have lost, while other guides serve as fact finders, researching the information you are seeking and bringing it to you when you need it most. Spirit guides come in all shapes, sizes, and species. Some of the guides that I have seen for people range from Yale professors, to ancient wise women, to mermaids, fairies, and Atlantians. So give your imagination some credit for what it can see, and don't discount a guide just because he or she didn't come in the package you expected.

The focus of this meditation is to introduce you to a healing guide who can aid you in understanding where you might be holding dis-ease and how you can get it back in flow. As you go through the exercise, it is perfectly fine if you feel like you are not getting a clear picture of your guide. It takes time to develop these types of relationships, but eventually they will become familiar.

It is important that as you open up to working with other spirit-based energies, you remember that you are ultimately the final authority. If something doesn't feel right to you with a guide, then don't do it. The same goes if you don't like the guide who first comes to you; simply ask another guide to come in until you find one you are comfortable with and with whom you have a mutual respect. That said, what I have found of spirit guides is that they are very honoring and hold no judgment over us or others. Their messages are loving, gentle, and often amusing. However, your spirit guides will never tell you what to do; they will simply help you better understand and manage what you have designed for yourself. You are the authority in command simply because you have taken on the more difficult chore of hosting a body.

In this meditation, you will be performing a task called "plugging in," in which your healing guide will plug his or her hands into your hands and you will receive a healing. Notice that you are only letting your guide plug into your hands, not into your body. Allowing another spirit to enter your body is a process known as channeling, which is not covered in the scope of this book, nor is it necessary when seeking inner wisdom and balance. The reason for meeting a healing guide is to give you a conduit for understanding illness and learning how to heal yourself.

Focus Point:
Get In Your Reading Space

1. Begin this exercise by first performing the basic energy run. Ground, release, fill in, run earth and spirit currents to activate your chakras, and then finishing by defining your space with your rose boundaries.

2. Once you have consciously generated your field and given it protection, move into your center-of-head room and let yourself get comfortable.

3. Be sure to set your crown on neutrality and amusement, as you will want to be very open to

seeing, sensing, hearing, and knowing all about
your guide.

1. From your center-of-head room, notice a door on
   the right side of your room. This door leads out into
   a hallway that will take you into another room. The
   other room will serve as a common ground that will
   host your meeting. Feel yourself moving toward
   the door and begin to wander down the hallway,
   stopping when you see an opening. This is the
   meeting room.
2. As you step into the meeting room, allow your
   imagination to acclimate to your surroundings.
   Notice the condition of the room and how it makes
   you feel, and then find a place where both you and
   your guide can get comfortable.
3. Finally, speak out to the space around you, letting
   spirit know that you wish to meet your healing
   guide now.
4. Your healing guide will enter the room first as a ball
   of light. Watch for the orb as it floats into the space,
   noticing its color and radiance. Watch as the sphere
   hovers over the space you have provided for it.
5. As the orb hovers before you, explore your first
   impressions by sensing if the energy has a feminine
   or masculine essence. Once you have a sense of
   gender, allow the ball to start morphing into the
   shape and stature of your guide.
6. Watch as your guide takes on more and more
   definition and form. Look down at his or her feet,

and notice the types of shoes he or she is wearing, and ask yourself what that says about him or her.

7. Then continue to scan up the body being aware of what clothes your guide is wearing, and what that indicates about him or her. Also, take note of your guide's hair and eye color, noticing specifics.

8. Start to have a conversation with your guide. Ask him or her their name and how long they have been working with you as a guide. Ask him or her what he or she did when they lived as a spirit in a body and why they now want to be a guide to you. You may not get all the information you are looking for, but in time, your guides will validate their presence in your life. For now, concentrate on the healing.

FOCUS POINT:
HEALING WITH A GUIDE

1. Stand up and allow your guide to come and stand to either side of you. Put your hands out in front of you and sense the way your hands feel. Sense their density, shape, and the way they move.

2. Then ask your guide to "plug in" to your hands, from the wrists to the fingertips. Notice the sensations in your hands now that your healing guide is plugged in. How do your hands feel different? Do they move the same? Are they heavier, lighter, colder or hotter? Simply take note of the difference between your hands, and your hands superimposed with your guide's hands. Then ask your guide to unplug, again noticing the difference.

3. Have your guide plug in again. This time you can ask for a healing. Allow your healing guide to place your

hands, and his or hers, anyplace on your body that needs healing at this moment. Notice where your guide wants to take you; perhaps you need healing on your knee, shoulder, or heart. See if you can determine where the energy is residing in your space. Is it in your masculine, feminine, physical, mental, emotional, spiritual bodies; lower or higher mind; past, present, future, or archetypal self? It's ok if you don't get all your answers—in time, the process gets easier. For now, allow your guide to show you where your energy needs healing. Let him or her help you remove, or extract, any energy that is stuck or stagnant in your field. Take this time to enjoy the healing you are receiving. Watch as your healing guide shows you how to release the energy out into the universe or down your grounding cord where it will be healed, or transmuted, back to pure potential.

4. When your healing guide has completed your healing, have him or her disconnect from your hands. As he or she unplug, thank him or her for his or her service and let him or her know you look forward to further interactions.

5. As you leave the room, come back to your center-of-head room and then exit your inner exploration.

Remember that you have several guides, so get to know a few. Know that your guides are with you whenever you need them, and you can receive a healing at any time. Also know that these relationships can, and should, be fostered in your outward reality as well. Speak openly to your guides and begin to develop this relationship into a working friendship, just like you would do with anyone else.

16

How to
Become
Empowered

There once was a King who loved his daughter more than life itself. When the day came for his daughter to find a husband, the King knew not just any man would do. And so the King devised a plan that would ensure his daughter would always be in good hands. Whenever a suitor would come to call, the King would ask him only one question, "What is the one thing a woman wants most of all?" Only the man who could answer correctly would receive the King's most cherished gift. And so it was that the suitors came to call. One by one the King asked his question. Some answered money, while others guessed love, but these were not the answers to the King's curious riddle.

One day, a man came calling. He admitted to the King that at first he was perplexed by the question, for he did not know the answer. So the man set out to search the world in hopes of solving the King's encrypted puzzle. In the end, it was a woman herself who enlightened the man, giving him the answer he so diligently sought. Quickly, the man returned to his kingdom ready to enlighten his King with the answer to his question. It was then that the man whispered to the King, "The one thing a woman wants most of all is to be in charge of herself." The King was pleased. The man had passed the test and was worthy of his daughter. As a reward, the man and the King's daughter would live in love and in union all the rest of their days.

I believe that it is a fundamental nature within all of us, men and women, to want to be in charge of ourselves and to live freely and independently, in love with life and each other. In order to be free and independent, we first have to learn how to claim our experiences, speak our truths, listen to our intuition, and embody our higher beliefs. Once we can do these things efficiently, we are truly free, in charge, and empowered to create a world that mirrors our higher ideal. Nobody gives us the right to be in charge of ourselves; rather, we have to claim the right to be empowered.

The Fundamental Truth of Empowerment

Many years ago, I worked in the oil and gas industry and was employed by what was one of the largest petroleum corporations in the world at the time. I was a single mother then, and was working out of necessity rather than desire. Over the many years that I spent in this corporate environment, I came to realize one thing: my employer only saw me as a number. Additionally, the product we were producing for public use was also only about the number and had nothing to do with the people (let alone the planet).

When I realized that my employer had no concern for the planet or me as an individual, I felt offended, used, and betrayed. When I was hired, they said they were looking for outside-the-box thinkers, yet when I thought outside of the box, I was reprimanded and continuously denied my opportunity to do something different. After several unsuccessful attempts at changing the structure, I found myself in a difficult predicament. I was becoming argumentative, and extremely vocal about how I felt the corporation didn't really want change. They wanted lackeys who would keep their mouths shut and do as they were told. I suddenly found myself faced with the choice to either comply or leave.

Deciding whether or not to leave my position meant having to weigh the consequences of having a paycheck or not. If I stayed, I would have a mediocre but steady income, guaranteed. If I left, I might not be able to find something that paid the same, let alone an actual job. Like I said, I was a single mother. I was the sole provider for my home. Was it really in my best interest to quit the job that was meeting the financial needs of my family? Was I willing to enslave myself to get a paycheck for the sake of my children? Of course I was willing to sacrifice for my children, but to what end? It was one thing to sacrifice my personal soul, but it was another thing to consciously contribute to the ill-intended degradation of our earth, her resources, and the whole of humanity. I felt the cost of such a sacrifice would eventually trickle down to my children, grandchildren, and great grandchildren, and doom them to a life of uncertainty, poverty, oppression, and war. In the end, I chose to leave. The investment was too high a cost to justify the meager returns. I knew in my gut and my heart that the oil corporation's philosophy was fundamentally misguided, and what this company was perpetuating would only have negative results for humanity and the earth in the long run.

The sad thing was, even though I found another corporation where I could exhibit my outside-the-box thinking skills, their business model was exactly the same as the other; it was a different industry, but the same philosophy. The expectation was that I learn to smile and nod and keep my opinions to myself. It seemed that much of corporate America conducted business under the ideal of profit before people and planet. To say the least, I was disillusioned. I grew up hearing that all I had to do was be willing to work hard to earn a living and America would support my dream. Yet no one ever said that also meant turning a blind eye to the blatant disregard for the very people and resources that provided the profit in the first place. What kind of life is that?

As a child, I couldn't change the educational structure to accommodate my needs. As an adult, I couldn't change corporate America to accommodate my beliefs. But once again, I could use my inner wisdom to reinvent my personal circumstances by being in charge of myself, enacting my entrepreneurial nature, and learning to work for myself. In doing so, my spirit was once again teaching me that I had all the answers inside myself, and that I could create whatever I wanted by simply following my creative passion and living my personal truth.

How often do we stand up and say, "This is what I believe!"? How often do we really speak what is on our minds? How often do we consciously follow our gut instincts? The goal today is to become aware of the fundamental truth of our empowerment. We are only empowered once we can claim our authenticity and live the truth of our reality.

The Energetic Climate of Authenticity

What are your dreams and ideals? Are you cultivating the passion inside you? Think about the relationships in your life. Are you able to be your authentic self with family, friends, and coworkers? Where are you holding yourself back from showing the world who you are?

It is said that a person's power lies in his or her dreams, visions, and ideals. Should these powers go uncultivated, the person becomes merely a superior kind of beast, but when fostered, the person becomes enlightened and can sustain enlightened leadership.

As a nation facing a plethora of crises, it is authenticity that is prescribed as the magic pill that can cure all our ills. Yet the greatest benefit to the authenticity drug is not merely its ability to heal our personal circumstances, the authenticity drug also carries the side effect of empowerment that leads to reform. Finally, there is a drug that can cure all our physical, emotional, mental, spiritual, social, philosophical, and economic ills. The best part is that it's free and changes everything.

The only true power today comes from living authentically. In order to be authentic, you need to seek clarity regarding whose expectations you have been living up to and why. What are the expectations in your life? Are you expected to be a good student, wife, or employee? Whose expectation is it? Your mother's, husband's, or employer's? More importantly, can you tell the difference between the expectations you have of yourself versus the expectations everyone else has of you? You may very well want to be a good student, but if you are doing it because it appeases someone else's idea of what you should be, then you are not consciously enacting your authenticity. If you are striving to be a good student because you know that's who you are and not just who you are conditioned to be, then you are living from authenticity.

When you don't enact your authenticity, your life never seems real. You doubt that you know how to be a good mother, you doubt that you know what is best for yourself, and you doubt that you know how to love another. Yet, until you claim the right to know these things for yourself, outside of other people's expectations, you won't really know what you, yourself, think and believe. Remember, it is your thoughts and beliefs that influence what you create as experiences in your life. If you feel like you are going through the motions, merely existing, and not really living, then authenticity is the cure that will bring you back to life.

Technique:
Taking Back Your Power

Learning the difference between your authentic nature and the expectations of others begins by recognizing where you give your energy away, and where you take energy from others. Clairvoyantly, you can view this give-and-take as a cord. Cords energetically connect people (and things) to other people, like a cord between a mother and a child. Cords connect throughout the chakras in various ways. For instance, if a person's chakra needs something it thinks it doesn't have for itself, that person's chakra will send out a cord connecting to someone else's chakra, taking the energy needed as the person being corded begins giving his or her energy away. Yet you cannot just cord another person without his or her permission. Or can you? Unfortunately, most people are unconscious of their energetic exchanges and connections and have no idea what they are agreeing to and how they are influenced every day.

Because society is largely uneducated about its spirit, cords have become the standard mode of operating and getting your needs met. The purpose for these connections is varied; for instance, a husband and wife might share a cord between their fourth chakras of unconditional love. However, that same couple may also have a cord that goes from the woman's second chakra of sexuality and creativity to the man's third chakra of power and will. If the cord between their second and third chakras was initiated by the man, he might be taking his wife's ability to create for herself, and inadvertently disempowering her. If the cord had been initiated by the woman, she might be taking away her husband's power and leaving him unable to create anything new. You can see where the unconditional love cord is not a problem. However, the other cord becomes an issue when either the woman feels oppressed or the man feels trapped, at which time unconditional love gets lost in the mix.

Are you aware of your cords? Where do you give and take from the people in your life? You have cords with your family, friends, and even acquaintances that represent the agreements you have with whomever you are connected. The only concern with cords is that if you are unaware of the exchange of energy, you may be contributing to something unhealthy and codependent, or you may be denying yourself the right to sustain your own personal need. The truth is that there is no need to give away your own energy, nor is it necessary to take energy from others. We each have our own quantum field and everything that we need is in that field. We simply have to know how to access our own information. Knowing your cords and how they are serving you is your next step in claiming more of your personal space and authentic face.

In this exercise, you will explore the concept of cords and how to release them. Releasing cords is a relatively simple process; however, it is necessary to mention that some cords will naturally re-establish themselves even after you have disconnected them. For instance, when I teach a class and we are renewing our energy, I tell my students to release any cords that exist between them and everyone and everything (kids, jobs, and bills included). I tell them to let go of their children, significant others, friends, family, even pets, because it is necessary to know your energy field separate from everyone else's. However, even though they are releasing their cords in class, the minute the students think about, or enter into, the things that they have released, the cords will re-establish. The minute a mother thinks of her child, the cord is re-established. The minute you think about your work project, you re-establish your cord.

The only time a cord will not re-initiate is if you have consciously released the cord and changed your relationship to the situation that created it. For instance, should a women notice that the original cord still existed between her and her mother, she could release the cord, thereby freeing herself from her mother's need to parent her adult child. However, the cord will only stay detached should the woman foster her new position by no longer allowing her mother to impose her will and expectations on her. Instead, the woman would have to take the steps necessary for enacting her own truth regardless of her mother's opinion, setting a new standard within the relationship that no longer allowed a child-like type of cording. So you can release a cord, but you still have to change the behavior that allowed it in the first place.

FOCUS POINT:
GET IN YOUR SPACE AND BE NEUTRAL
1. Begin this exercise by first performing the basic energy run. Ground, release, fill in, and run earth and spirit currents to activate your chakras. Finish by putting your rose boundaries around you and keeping yourself protected.
2. Once you have consciously generated your field, move into your center-of-head room and let yourself get comfortable.
3. To prepare for this reading, be sure to set your crown on neutrality and amusement.
4. Once you set your crown, pull down your reading screen and activate it with your sixth and seventh chakras.

FOCUS POINT:
VIEWING YOUR ENERGETIC CORDS
1. Think of someone or something in your life that you might be having a difficult time with. Put an image of yourself and the other person (or thing) up on your reading screen and take as much time as you need to observe the cord(s) that is creating the difficulty.

2. Pay attention to the size of the cord, its color, and whether the energy is flowing from you to the other person, vice versa, or both.

3. Observe which chakras the cord is connected to and why. Below is a quick reminder about the chakras and what they maintain so you can better investigate why the cord exists:

   a. The first chakra regulates your sense of safety, security, home, and money.

   b. The second chakra regulates the emotions, creativity, sexuality, passion, and desire.

   c. The third chakra regulates our power, will, and force.

   d. The fourth chakra regulates our capacity for love of self, love of others, and love of life.

   e. The fifth chakra regulates our ability to communicate the truth of ourselves both inwardly and outwardly.

   f. The sixth chakra regulates your ability to think intellectually and connect with your spirit and higher intuitive sense.

   g. The seventh chakra regulates your connection to the Divine as well as your ability to live your most authentic face.

4. Ask yourself the following questions as you observe the energy exchange of your cord:

   a. Why am I giving or taking this energy?

   b. What are the consequences of this energy exchange in my life?

   c. Why am I agreeing to have this exchange?

   d. Is this cord helping or hindering me?

e. How can I help myself?

f. Do I want to keep this cord or release it?

5. Once you have taken some time to examine the reason for the cord, you can release the cord if you feel it is not in your best interest.

6. To release the cord, simply watch yourself take hold of the cord and unplug it from your space, sending it back to the other party and allowing that person to rectify his or her difference too. Although the other person may not be conscious of this disconnect, his or her spirit will be conscious of it and will help his or her physical and mental bodies integrate the new agreement.

7. After releasing, fill in the hole where the cord once was with a golden sun.

8. When you are finished, bring your attention back to your center-of-head room, turning off your reading screen and disconnecting from the process.

Take the next several days to contemplate what you have discovered in this meditation and seek more insight if needed. Notice how the themes of this cord relate to your physical reality, and then notice how things are different as a result of having performed this exercise. Don't forget to enact new behaviors based on what you observed.

17

How
to Change

Jane wanted a change more than anything in the world. She worked long hours in her high-tech career, took care of her emotionally fragile mother, and was raising her son all by herself. But Jane didn't believe in complaining. She was brave and she put on a brave face, living up to her responsibilities without ever wavering. Still, Jane dreamed of a day when her life would be different. She yearned for the freedom to come and go as she wanted, and she longed for the day she could find a love of her own. However, because Jane never spoke of her desires, the change she was seeking could never come.

Then one day Jane snapped. She put her foot down with her boss, demanding a raise to go with all her extra hours; she stopped coddling to her mother's insecurities; and she began assigning tasks to her son to help out around the house. Before Jane knew it, everything had changed. Her boss valued her worked and the two came to a mutual agreement on her new salary. Jane's mother started managing the bills and cooking all the meals. Jane's son proudly assisted his mother, taking pride in his ability to do things for himself. Before long Jane found that her life had completely transformed. But more importantly, Jane had just found the key to always being able to create the changes she desired in her life.

Prior to Jane putting her foot down, she was unable to transform her reality because she was strictly internalizing her dreams. Jane would ponder to herself the idea of a life worth living but she would never speak of her desires with anyone. However, the minute Jane did finally communicate her need for change outwardly, her reality immediately followed suit. Change doesn't happen simply because we want it to. Change happens when we claim the experiences we wish to see by speaking our desires into existence. Like Mahatma Gandhi said, "You must be the change you wish to see in the world." Jane had spoken her desires into existence and changed her reality into the world she wished to see.

The Fundamental Truth of Change

Communication is the key to outward manifestation. In the previous story of Skip's healing and life transformation, it wasn't until he communicated to the world his creative self-expression that his reality truly changed. The minute Skip began telling people of his invention, he began receiving support for his idea, which ultimately led to the sustainable change he was seeking. If we only ponder and stew over our desires but never outwardly express them, then we are in effect telling the magnetizing forces of the universe to keep our desires only as inward fantasies. However, if we communicate what we desire outwardly to the physical world, we are telling the magnetizing forces to manifest our desires in our physical reality.

Healing happens when we inwardly take conscious charge over our total needs emotionally, physically, mentally, and spiritually, and follow the path that is unique to our individuality. Empowerment happens when we take charge over our expectations and are brave enough to live authentically. Change happens when we openly and outwardly communicate our higher truths and are willing to create the world of our dreams.

The Energetic Climate
of Certainty versus Validation

One thing I always tell my clients is when you begin communicating your desires outwardly in the world, be selective with whom you are confiding. Not everyone needs to know everything you are doing. And not everyone will be supportive of your dreams. When I began writing this book, I first only told the people I knew would be supportive as I didn't want to set myself up for failure. Rather than wholly opening myself up to everyone's rhetoric about my desires, I reserved my communications for only a select few whose rhetoric I knew would be positive and supportive. I had enough insecurities of my own and I didn't need other people telling me how I couldn't do it. Instead, I needed the people who would cheer me on and who had confidence in my ability so I could gain my own certainty for seeing the project to fruition.

At some point in the process, your dreams are going to become your reality and everyone will know your desires regardless of whether you think they can accept them or not. When you begin openly communicating your truth in the world, you need to feel a certain level of confidence in what you are espousing. In that sense, you have to believe you can manifest your desires. While the support of others is comforting, your certainty is what ultimately determines your reality's outcome. In that sense, it doesn't matter if someone validates your ideas or not because you have certainty and can validate yourself.

Certainty comes from not second guessing your inner wisdom. The truth is that we all know what is right for us individually and never need anyone else to validate our beliefs. Outward validation is nice, but not necessary. When you rely on the validation from others to determine the course of your life, you are letting other people take charge of your reality.

However, having certainty doesn't mean it's your way or the highway. Having certainty means knowing what you believe, why you believe it, and that you can live your truth while allowing others to live their truths, too.

Do you feel comfortable making decisions on your own? Or do you need others to tell you what is in your best interest? A good way to gauge your certainty is to determine how much you can validate yourself that you are on your path versus how much you need the reassurance and validation from others. If you feel you cannot make a change in your life without someone else approving it, then validation is keeping you down and you need to learn to validate yourself. However, if you are open to listening to the ideas of others but know you will ultimately determine the best course of action for yourself, then validation only serves to reinforce what you already know.

Technique:
Sparking Creativity

In order to enact change today, you need to know how to spark a new creative intention. Most people want change, but they don't know what that change should be. When you don't have a specific idea about what you want to create new in your life, taking up a creative pursuit becomes your path to inspiration and change. When you work at something creative, you rev up your creative forces and intuitive mind, and suddenly new ideas begin to flow. One of these ideas is going to be the something new you are looking to create. The truth is that inspiration comes to us every day. Unfortunately, most of us are not listening or generating the necessary creative forces to attract us to what we don't know we are looking for. The following exercise is designed to help you get your creative juices flowing so your spirit can send you an inspired idea.

FOCUS POINT:
SPARKING YOUR CREATIVITY

1. The best way to rev up or increase your creative capacity is to take up a simple and meaningless creative endeavor. For example, if you want a new career but don't know what you want to do, take a painting class, bead, put together a puzzle, or any creative endeavor, and during this activity, simply allow your creative self to open up so you can receive a spark of inspiration.

2. The creative pursuit you choose doesn't matter. It is simply that you send a signal to the quantum field that says you wish to partake in a new creative endeavor.

3. It also doesn't matter if you do anything with your creative projects, because it isn't about producing a product for someone else. It's about sparking your inspiration so you can come to know just what you want for yourself.

4. If you are looking for something new, start taking on a creative project. Before long, you will find an idea worth following.

5. The only other thing you have to do is be willing and brave enough to follow the spark you initiated.

Technique:
Setting Intentions

Change happens with intention and communication. If you recall, the most powerful part of your human DNA is your ability to consciously set intentions. We have all heard the saying, "Ask and it is given." It is in the asking that you are magnetizing your intentions. But all too often we ask from a place of a place of not having, or lack, and that's why we never "get." What I mean is that generally people set their intentions and speak to the universe about their desires to have more money or things. Yet this type of asking usually comes from lack in the sense that we feel we either didn't have these things growing up or we don't have them now and that is why we want; to compensate for originally not having. When you create your reality based on lack, your future is not sustainable because by definition there is not enough to support growth. Money and things cannot be a goal because they are rewards. Money follows the cycle of time. If you look at where the wealth of money is today, only 1 percent of the earth's population actually has an abundance of this resource. This is because the cycle we have been in is one of profit over people and planet. This is why artists starve and executives make millions. What we learn with this cycle is that it really goes against most people's nature to put profit above relationships, which is why the other 99 percent of us seemingly have a lack of money. The good news is that with the new world age shift today, the cycle is changing to one of people and planet before profit. That means that over the next several years, money will start to flow toward those who value their relationship and the planet before personal agenda. But the point is that setting intentions has nothing to do with money, however, that is what we mostly ask to be given. So maybe start intending to value your relationships more and watch and see what happens to your finances.

I suggest that when you think about setting intentions and creating your life, you understand that there are many experiences that you can have that will enrich your life and give you what you are truly seeking. Maybe set intentions to:

1. Embrace a new quantum education

2. Balance your many selves

3. Recognize the Divine in everyone

4. Reconcile karma and forgive the past

5. Remember your soul's history

6. Claim your own beliefs

7. Follow the truth of your spirit

8. Find the courage to live authentically

9. Speak your heart openly with others

10. Change with the cycle of time

11. Honor your body and spirit

12. Take charge of your energies to create

13. Meet new people

14. Partake in new experiences

This list is endless. Feel free to intend what you wish, but just keep in mind that all of your intentions will bring you the rewards you are seeking, not just physically with money, but emotionally, mentally, and spiritually as well. Through intending that you be balanced on all these levels, you are creating a holistic environment in which you can sustainably flourish.

The first key to consciously setting an intention is to recognize your internal dialogue and what you believe about what you are asking for. If you are asking for a book deal, does your internal dialogue believe you are worthy of it? If your inner talk doesn't match your outward desire, then the intention is likely not to manifest. If your inner talk is certain and confident, then it is likely that your intention will at some point manifest into your reality. The first thing to consider when setting intentions isn't the intention itself, it's about first recognizing what you believe about what you desire. Maybe the first intention anyone should set is the intention to listen more to their internal conversations, as it is our thoughts that create reality.

Setting intentions is a simple process. You can do it in any way you prefer. When I was in clairvoyant school, we learned a process called "mock ups." In a sense, we would intend what we wanted to get out of the class, and we would put it out to the universe and watch and see how it came to us during our lessons. Since then, I have adapted my intention-setting process to better fit my need. Below is an example of how I teach others to set intentions. It is based on what I do for myself, but I encourage you to find what works best for you.

> FOCUS POINT:
> SETTING INTENTIONS
> 1. Setting intentions doesn't require that you be in your center-of-head room and you don't have to be running your energy to make it work; these things can help focus your energy better, but are not necessary.
> 2. Simply close your eyes, or intend that your consciousness be projected inward, and start to form a picture of what you wish to experience in your life. If you want more clarity, see yourself understanding the bigger picture and get a sense of how you feel emotionally in that state of knowingness.
> 3. The biggest key to manifesting an intention is the amount of emotional charge you generate around what you are defining. If you are not emotionally elated about your desires, then the emotional charge is weak and will have a difficult time harnessing the

energy to manifest itself. There is a phenomenon in life that happens when we are emotionally charged; we suddenly have the abilities to create miracles instantly. I've heard stories of women who have lifted vehicles off their children in a time of crisis. The emotional charge one must have to muster that much energy is enormous, but it makes sense when you think about a mother and how she feels about her child.

4. Let your emotions charge your intention. If you are feeling it, then it is a true desire. If you are not feeling it, you may not really want what you think you want, or you may not believe you can have it. Either way, go back to your internal dialogue and listen again to what you want and what part of you is in charge of that desire. Ask yourself if they are in alignment.

5. Once you have given vision to your desire, and you have magnetized it with your emotions, protect your desire by putting it in a bubble, or a geometric sphere.

6. I like to add energy into the sphere that I think will help it. For instance, if I am intending that my sons be safe and protected in a bubble for themselves, I will expand their bubbles, giving them plenty of room to do what they need to do for themselves, and then I will ask that the angels and our family members surround the bubble, lending it unconditional love and support to further keep them safe and protected.

7. Last, I like to give my bubble of intention a color, something that represents its overall essence. That color is always unique and individual to the intent. If the intent is for seeing the Divine in everyone, I might use a bright white to light up my sphere of intention. If the intent is to attract a new career, I might use a metallic blue to light up my intention. Pick any color that works for you in regard to your intention.

8. Once you have defined, protected, and set the color of your intention, simply toss it out into the universe so it can magnetize to you what you desire. There is no need to check in on your bubble, and you can recreate it at anytime, but the more you can be detached from expecting it on a certain timeframe, the more you empower it with your faith in Divine timing. Sometimes intending to be more detached from expectations is a necessary intention, too.

9. The only other thing you need to do is watch for your intention to manifest. This can be tricky, because it doesn't always come in the exact package you visualized. Rather, the central-organizing force of the universe will attract like-minded people and events your way. You simply have to determine which people and events match your intentions, as these things will lead you to your desires. This means not being afraid to follow coincidences, or synchronicities, and instead sparking up conversations with the people you encounter. I personally think our intentions are manifesting daily, but we are too closed off to the people around us to see that they have our answers.

We are all each other's answers. If we recall what consciousness researcher Lynne McTaggart said about the quantum field, "We are attached and engaged, indivisible from our world and our only fundamental truth is our relationship with it." The fundamental truth is that reality happens when we engage in relationships either with others or merely with the circumstances of our lives. If we are afraid of having friends, being real with our family, experiencing intimacy with another, or if we are fearful of seeking a new career or way of life then we are denying ourselves the opportunities to allow our intentions to be attracted to us. This book is about healing and balancing your individual self. But it is also about remembering that we all need each other—today more than ever.

In closing with the techniques, let them become a part of your everyday life. If you are at work, set the space of your office, intend how you wish to be and what you wish to experience for your day, be neutral to those around you, and check in with your energy throughout the day. Fill in with a sun when you need it, get your earth and sprit energies moving, and clear out anything that gets in your way. Listen to yourself and consult your higher knowing while you are sitting in a meeting. Understand your rhetoric and agenda for what you are speaking, and speak the truth of yourself. We are integrating our spirits with our bodies; they are one in the same. Let your clairvoyant self become a natural part of your every day living.

Conclusion:
The New American Dream

*We are such stuff as dreams are made on, and our little life
is rounded with a sleep.*

—William Shakespeare, *The Tempest*

Shakespeare knew full well that it is in the dreaming where reality is
forged. It is for that reason alone that dreaming is by far our greatest
gift. In my years of personal research and study, I have come to learn that
America was once formed on a dream, but not the dream we are familiar
with in which hard work is the key to bettering yourself, but the dream
of the ancient philosophers. She was founded on an ancient vision con-
ceptualized by the great philosophers to one day be a seed for universal
democracy in which all nations would cooperate in a commonwealth of
states. In the dream, all matters of human need—physically, mentally,

emotionally, and spiritually—would be met through systems of education, philosophy, and social conduct. From there, the states would operate under a self-rule understanding, as the people would be properly educated to know the right actions by which to govern themselves. In the philosophical American Dream, the commonwealth would prosper, both by personal gain as well as collectively contributing to supporting the needs of one another. And in the dream, America would be setting the example in the world for what could be achieved when a nation nurtures the needs of its people and unites them under an acceptance of all beliefs.

If this sounds like utopia, it is. Unfortunately, not many people today believe utopia is a rational possibility. However, the only reason we consider a utopian society to be irrational and impractical is because we ourselves are fundamentally uneducated regarding the full scope of our own human need. If we were properly educated, utopia wouldn't seem so outlandish; rather, it would feel more like second nature and a Divine right. The original dream of America is fully within our grasp today. However, in order for this dream to come true, all manners of the human need and condition must be considered and incorporated into our educational, philosophical, and social systems.

It is widely known that the youth of today are not expected to outlive their parents' generation, nor is it likely that they will have the resources necessary to sustain our ways of being. However, there are free technologies and higher sciences available to us today that can absolutely prove the statistics wrong. The lesser task we have before us today is the reconstructing and reorganizing of our political, economic, and social systems. The greater challenge we have today is re-educating ourselves about who we are as spiritual beings living a human existence. Yet it is our greater challenge that makes our lesser task simpler, if not moot. Our structures around education, insurance, health care, media, and government certainly all need to be reinvented today. You just have to watch television to know that these systems are not holding up anymore. Teachers are picketing the content of their text books, insurance companies deny coverage to people who need it most under the clause of pre-existing conditions, health care for most is nonexistent, and the media focuses on propaganda while our government officials misuse our money to promote their personal and corporate agendas. However, before we can reorganize our structures into sustainable systems, humanity must first learn to sustain its soul lest our re-organizations serve merely as a bandage and not a cure.

That we are physical is obvious, but that we are mental, emotional, and spiritual beings housed within a soul is not so obvious; these elements require closer examination and consideration as part of the total need of an individual. Until we begin to educate our culture about the hidden natures of living as a spirit in a body, no policy we reconstruct will sustain.

We all have a unique challenge and opportunity today to radically alter the ways in which we live our lives. Part of our alteration begins by embracing a higher science that takes into consideration the total human condition. The other part of our alteration begins by reconnecting to our magic, or that which is our ability to imagine a new reality into being. Once we have met these challenges of learning a higher education and finding the power within, we can bring consciousness and wisdom into our everyday ways of being. With these resolves, our social, political, and economic issues could solve themselves with innovative and visionary solutions.

In a time of abounding prophecies, predictions, and assumptions, I have found only one piece of literature that clearly states the purpose of the times. In 1944, philosopher and sage Manly P. Hall wrote an article titled "The Origin of the Democratic Ideal." He said,

These are the days of Americans' opportunity to lead a still-troubled mankind toward a better way of life. If we meet this challenge, we will ensure not only the survival of our nation for centuries to come, but we shall gain the enduring gratitude of our fellow men and Americans will be remembered to the end of time as a great enlightened people.

As Americans we have an amazing opportunity today to reinvent a new standard of living that takes into consideration the greatest good of all. All we have to ask ourselves is how we want the generations to remember us. Do we want them to remember us as a people who took and gave nothing back? Or do we want them to remember us as innovators who used the power of their spirits to bring the philosophical dream of America into reality? While sustainability in the physical comes from living locally and supporting local community members, businesses, and products, sustainability in spirit comes from following our hearts and enacting our free creative expression. The time is now to exercise our freedom. Can we free our wills and liberate our minds into seeking insightful solutions? Can we use our free expression to conceive new ideas and change our personal status quo? Not only can we, but we must if we desire to grow into the magnificent people and nation we are destined to become.

Bibliography

Bostwick, Lewis, Berkley Psychic Institute, accessed November 10, 2011, http://www.berkeleypsychic.com/ShowPage.asp?id=163.

Clark, Robert B. *The Four Gold Keys.* Newburyport: Hampton Roads Publishing, 2002.

"Desert Flower—The Movie." The Desert Flower Foundation, accessed November 10, 2011, http://www.waris-dirie-foundation.com/en/desert-flower-the-movie/press/.

Emoto, Masaru, and David A. Thayne. *The Hidden Messages in Water.* Hillsboro: Beyond Worlds Publishing, 2004.

Hall, Manly P. "The End of the Quest." In *The Secret Destiny of America.* New York: Penguin, 1944.

———. *The Secret Destiny of America.* New York: Penguin, 2008.

Ingerman, Sandra. *Soul Retrieval: Mending the Fragmented Self.* New York: HarperCollins, 1991.

Jenkins, John Major. *The 2012 Story: The Myths, Fallacies, and Truth Behind the Most Intriguing Date in History.* New York: Penguin, 2009.

Johnson, Robert A. *Inner Work: Using Dreams and Active Imagination for Personal Growth.* New York: HarperCollins, 1986.

Leininger, Bruce, Andrea Leininger, and. Ken Gross. *Soul Survivor: The Reincarnation of a World War II Fighter Pilot.* New York: Grand Central Publishing, 2009.

Lundeen, J.S., and A.M. Steinberg. "Experimental Joint Weak Measurement on a Photon Pair as a Probe of Hardy's Paradox." *Physical Review Letters*, 2004, 102: 020404–000001. doi:10.1103/PhysRevLett.102.020404.

McTaggart, Lynne. "The Coming Revolution." In *The Field: The Quest for the Secret Force of the Universe.* New York: HarperCollins, 2002.

Puryear, Herbert B. *The Edgar Cayce Primer: Discovering the Path to Self-Transformation.* New York: Bantam, 1982.